Patterns

Armistice Socks. 60
Bouncing Bunnies Socks. 22
Chicken Little Socks. 50
Dreaming of the Caribbean Socks. 19
Drifting Leaves Socks. 56
Fireworks Socks. 40
Hoarfrost Socks. 7
Honeybee Socks. 31
Honeycomb Tea Cozy. 38
It Never Stays In Vegas Socks. 44
Northern Lights Mitts. 17
Northern Lights Socks 13
Pushing Up Tulips Socks 27
Snowflake Christmas Stocking. 64

This book is dedicated to my mother for believing that I was capable enough to learn and do anything in this life, Tina Johnston for believing that I was a better knitter than I thought I was, Linda Leffler for her help in test knitting everything, Teresa Ruch who keeps pushing me to grow as an artist, and all of the knitters at BlackSheep at Orenco in Hillsboro, OR who helped make this book possible.

Text Copyright 2016 by Kelli Slack
Photographs Copyright 2016 by Monika Dechene
Modeled by Grace Johnston

Charts created with Intwined Pattern Studio

All Rights Reserved

Thank you for helping me to protect my work and support my pattern writing by refraining from reproducing any part of this book.

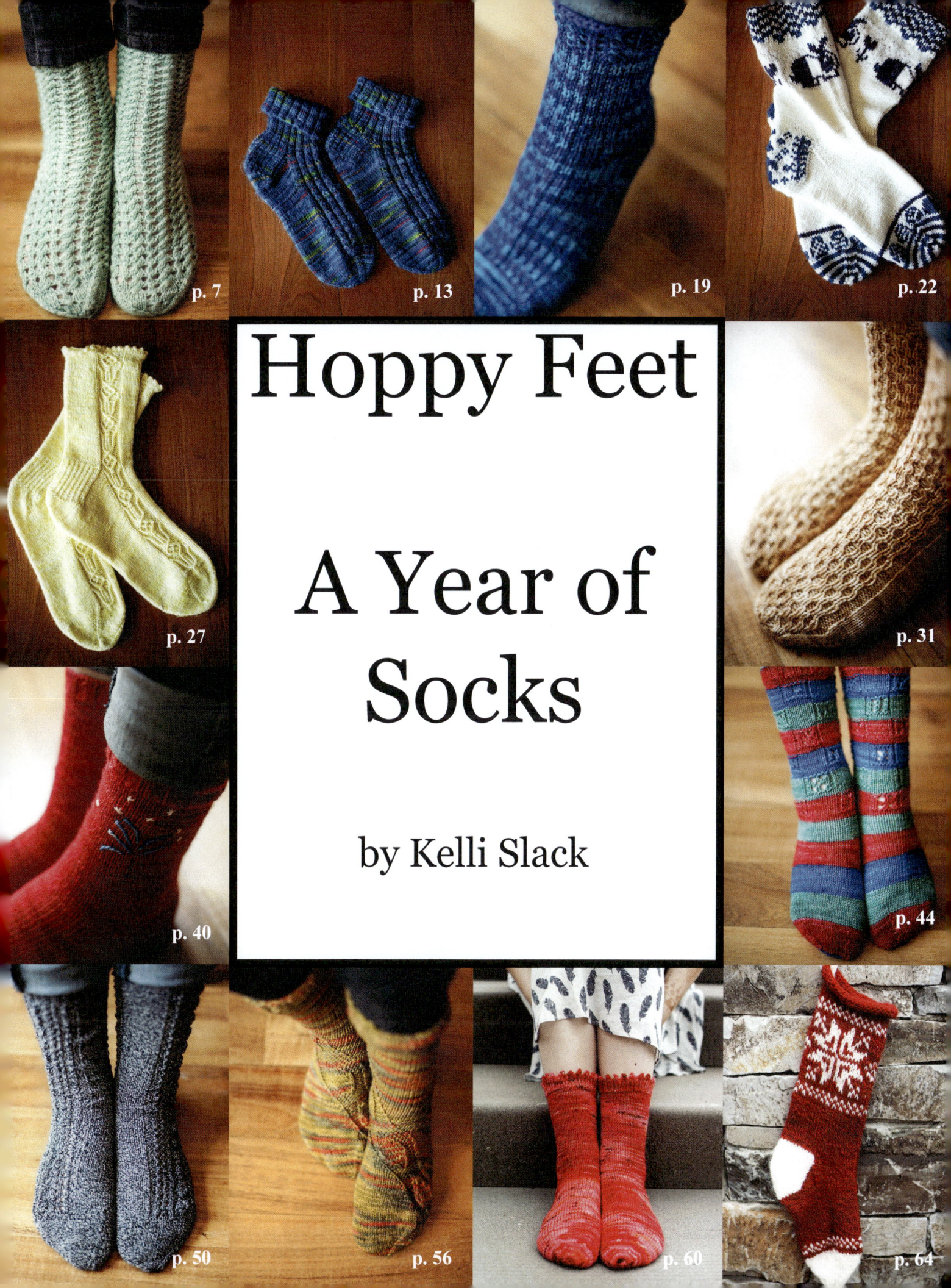

Hoppy Feet

A Year of Socks

by Kelli Slack

An Introduction: Using This Book

Welcome to Hoppy Feet. I hope you'll have a grand time as we explore heels, toes, pattern stitches, cast-ons, cast-offs, and the joy of socks. Each month's pattern will offer techniques that may be familiar or entirely new. The socks have been carefully designed to highlight a range of styles and techniques to carry you from a sock novice (or master) into mastery. Whether you are a long time sock knitter looking for a new challenge or a new sock knitter just starting your journey, I hope to offer you a joyous bounty of socks throughout the year.

This year of socks includes 12 sock designs, one for each month, and ranges from toe-up and top-down through calf-length socks, footies, and a Christmas stocking. In addition, two bonus patterns have been included to make your sock knitting journey a little more fun.

Some important points to consider while knitting socks:

~ socks may be knit in many ways, on double pointed needles, by magic loop, with two circulars
~ socks may be knit singly or two at a time, some may even be knit one inside the other
~ socks are always knit with negative ease, this means that the fabric must stretch to fit around the foot
~ negative ease will also keep socks from sliding down the calf
~ properly fit socks hug your foot to prevent wear and tear on the fabric
~ properly fit socks will not slide on your foot as you wear them
~ there are many different heels and toes and some will fit your foot better than others which is why we will try many different heels and toes
~ cast-offs (for toe-ups) and cast-ons (for top-downs) should be stretchy enough to fit around the leg; in other words, don't cast-on/off too tightly

My gauge:

_____ stitches per inch (spi)

x _____ circumference of foot
x 0.9 negative ease

= _____ ideal stitches

To calculate your gauge for each sock: make a small swatch (3 inches by 3 inches or so), measure your stitches per inch (spi), multiply your spi by the circumference of your foot. Then multiply this number by 0.9. This will give you a number for your ideal cast-on for the sock size you want to knit. The formula is included above.

Use the formula to check the fit of the sock you want to knit. If your cast-on number is close to your ideal stitches, then you are ready to knit. If your ideal number is different from the cast-on number, you will need to adjust your gauge to increase or decrease the circumference of the foot as needed.

Hoppy Feet ~ A Year of Socks

Techniques Used in This Book

Each month will have the techniques listed at the top of the pattern. Feel free to use these lists to mark the techniques as you learn and try them. When you have knit your way through the sock patterns, you will have checked off every one!

Toes

3-pointed Toe
Colorwork Wedge
Flat Toe
Increased 4-Point Toe
Pointed Toe
Wedge Toe

Cable and Lace Wedge
Contrast Toe
French Toe
Increased Wedge Toe
Star Toe
Wide Toe

Heels

Afterthought Heel
Cable and Lace Heel
Contrast Heel
German Heel
Short Row Heel
Toe-Up Round Heel

Band Heel
Colorwork Heel
French Heel
Reverse Slip Stitch Heel
Slip Stitch Heel
Welsh Heel

Cast-Ons/ -Offs

2-Color Braided Cast-On
Alternating Cable Cast-On
Chained-On Cast-On
Jenny's Surprisingly Stretchy Cast-Off
Judy's Magic Cast-On
Long Tail Cast-On
Picot Cast-On
Tillybuddy's Very Stretchy Cast-On
Twisted German Cast-On

Double Start Cast-On
Knitted-On Cast-On
Picot Hem Bind-Off
Turkish Cast-On

Other Techniques

Cables
Embroidery
Puff Stitch
Slipped Stitches
Textured Stitches
Top-Down Socks

Colorwork
Lace
Scalloped Cuff
Stacked Ribbing
Toe-Up Socks
Twisted Stitch Cables

Ranking the Socks

These socks vary greatly in their ease of knitting. I've ranked them here from easiest to hardest based on the techniques used.

The easiest socks are the Fireworks Socks.

1) Fireworks Socks
2) Armistice Socks
3) Northern Lights Socks
4) Dreaming of the Caribbean Socks
5) Snowflake Christmas Stocking
6) It Never Stays In Vegas Socks
7) Chicken Little Socks
8) Drifting Leaves Socks
9) Bouncing Bunnies Socks
10) Honeybee Socks
11) Pushing Up Tulips Socks
12) Hoarfrost Socks

The hardest socks are the Hoarfrost Socks.

Hoppy Feet ~ A Year of Socks

Hoarfrost Socks

January's Pattern: Hoarfrost Socks

Welcome to the first sock of the year! This sock may look daunting, but the secret is that you only have to pay attention to a pattern row once every four rounds. If you haven't tried a cable and lace sock before, you are in for a treat.

This first sock starts off with a Twisted German Cast-On which happens to be a favorite of mine. It is slightly more elastic than a Long-Tail Cast-On, but still has a tidy edge. The Twisted German Cast-On lends a stately turn to any sock cuff and keeps your stitches from wandering.

As we traverse the leg, a classic knit 1, purl 1 ribbed cuff gives way to a lace and cable pattern. Don't be fooled; the lace and cables are patterned on the same row with three "rest" rows in between. The combination of the four rows makes the leg pattern appear more difficult than it really is.

I wanted to continue the cable and lace pattern onto the heel, so choose to chart out a decreasing cable into the heel. The rest of the heel is a traditional Round heel with turned heel and gussets.

The cable and lace pattern continues down the top of the foot, culminating in a Patterned Wedge Toe. Like the heel, I carried the patterning down the toe and decreased for a Wedge Toe. Then the live stitches are grafted together using kitchener stitch.

The Hoarfrost socks were my sixth iteration of an idea to combine cables with lace. I made and rejected five other samples before settling on this pattern. It was not what I had originally envisioned, but I love it so much more.

Due to the nature of the cables and lace in this sock it is not a particularly stretchy sock. Knitters should take this into account when knitting this pattern.

Techniques

Twisted German Cast-On
Cable and Lace Patterned Heel
Patterned Wedge Toe
Cables
Lace

Skill level: This pattern is meant for an adventurous novice to intermediate knitter. Please read the entire pattern before beginning.

Yarn: 1 skein Madelinetosh Tosh Sock, 395 yards, Courbet is Green, 100% Merino Wool OR Black Trillium Merilon, 75% Superwash Merino and 25% Nylon, 425 yards, color Saltwater

Needle: US 1 (2.25 mm) Hiya Hiya Steel Double Pointed Needles (DPNs) or needles to obtain gauge

Gauge: 7.3 (7.4) stitches per inch (spi) and 9 (10) rows per inch (rpi) OR 29 (29.6) stitches & 36 (40) rows to 4 inches/10 cm in stockinette

Size: To fit a US women's 8.5-9 shoe, approx. 8.25" circumference and 9" foot

Abbreviations: See the back of the book.

Please note that this pattern is not stretchy due to the cables.

To Begin Socks:
Using the Twisted German Cast-on, cast-on 56 stitches. Join in the round, being careful not to twist. You may want to mark the beginning of your round with a stitch marker, bit of floss, or waste yarn.

Sock Cuff:
Row 1: *K1, P1, repeat from * until end of round.

Repeat row 1 until the cuff measures 1 inch in length.

Begin Leg:
Knit pattern repeat 8 times in each row.

Leg Pattern Chart Repeat:
Row 1: *k7, repeat from * to end of row
Row 2: *2/2rc, yo, sk2p, yo* repeat from * to * to end of row
Row 3: *k7, repeat from * to end of row
Row 4: *k7, repeat from * to end of row

Continue knitting the pattern repeat as established until leg measures 6 inches or to desired length. Slip all markers (if used) as you come to them. End on row 3 of the pattern repeat.

Heel Flap:
The heel is worked over the first 25 stitches of the row. Hold the remaining 31 stitches for the top of the foot.

Start Heel Flap:
Row 1 (rs): c3p1lc, k17, c3p1rc
Row 2 (ws): slip wyif, p24
Row 3 (rs): slip wyib, c3p1lc, k2, 2/2rc, yo, sk2p, yo, 2/2rc, k2, c3p1rc, k1
Row 4 (ws): slip wyif, k1, p21, k1, p1
Row 5 (rs): slip wyib, p1, c3p1lc, k13, c3p1rc, p1, k1
Row 6 (ws): slip wyif, k2, p19, k2, p1
Row 7 (rs): slip wyib, p2, c3p1lc, 2/2rc, yo, sk2p, yo, 2/2rc, c3p1rc, p2, k1
Row 8 (ws): slip wyif, k3, p17, k3, p1
Row 9 (rs): slip wyib, p3, c3p1lc, k9, c3p1rc, p3, k1
Row 10 (ws): slip wyif, k4, p15, k4, p1
Row 11 (rs): slip wyib, p4, c3p1lc, k2, yo, sk2p, yo, k2, c3p1rc, p4, k1
Row 12 (ws): slip wyif, k5, p13, k5, p1
Row 13 (rs): slip wyib, p5, c3p1lc, k5, c3p1rc, p5, k1
Row 14 (ws): slip wyif, k6, p11, k6, p1
Row 15 (rs): slip wyib, p6, c3p1lc, yo, sk2p, yo, c3p1rc, p6, k1
Row 16 (ws): slip wyif, k7, p9, k7, p1
Row 17 (rs): slip wyib, p7, c3p1lc, k1, c3p1rc, p7, k1
Row 18 (ws): slip wyif, k8, p7, k8, p1
Row 19 (rs): slip wyib, p8, 2/1lpc, k1, 2/rlpc, p8, k1
Row 20 (ws): slip wyif, k9, p5, k9, p1
Row 21 (rs): slip wyib, p9, t2l, k1, t2r, p9, k1
Row 22 (ws): slip wyif, k10, p3, k10, p1

Continue knitting heel flap as established, slipping the first stitch of each row until the heel flap measures 2 inches.

Heel Turn:
Row 1: S1, P10, K2, SSK, K1, turn work.
Row 2: S1, P2, P2tog, P1, turn work
Row 3: S1, Knit to one stitch before gap, SSK, K1, turn work.
Row 4: S1, Purl to one stitch before gap, P2tog, P1, turn work.

Repeat rows 3 & 4 until all of the stitches have been worked. On the last 2 rows, you will not have enough stitches to knit or purl the last stitch. Knit across row. There will be 13 stitches left.

Gusset:
Pick up and knit 13 stitches along heel flap, pm, continue working across the front leg stitches as established, pm, then pick-up and knit 13 stitches along the other side of the heel flap. Knit 6 stitches of heel turn, PM. This is now the beginning of the row.

On the next row, K17, K2tog, K1 SM, work pattern as established across top of foot, SM, K1, SSK, K16. On the next row, work pattern as established.

Continue gusset decreases:
Row A: Knit to 3 stitches before marker, K2tog, K1, SM, continue in leg pattern as established, SM, K1, SSK, knit to beginning of round marker.
Row B: Knit in pattern as established.

Repeat rows A & B until there are 56 stitches left.

Foot:
Continue knitting in established pattern until the foot measures 2 inches less than the total length of the foot (approx. 7 inches) or to desired length. End with row 3 of the leg pattern and do not knit the last 12 stitches of the row.

Toe:
Move the beginning of the round stitchmarker to between the patterned top of the foot and the bottom of the foot on the left side.

For the underside of the foot: ssk, knit until 2 stitches before the stitch marker on the other side of the sole, K2tog. Beginning with row 1 of the Toe Chart, knit in the new pattern across the top of the foot.

Continue knitting new pattern as established, decreasing the sole stitches on odd rows, and knitting across the sole stitches on even rows. At the end of the toe chart, there should be 14 stitches left.

Round 1: ssk, k1, c3o1l, k17, c3o1r, k1, k2tog
Round 2: k27
Round 3: ssk, k1, c3o1l, k2, 2/2rc, yo, sk2p, yo, 2/2rc, k2, c3o1r, k1, k2tog
Round 4: k25
Round 5: ssk, k1, c3o1l, k13, c3o1r, k1, k2tog
Round 6: k23
Round 7: ssk, k1, c3o1l, k4, yo, sk2p, yo, k4, c3o1r, k1, k2tog
Round 8: k21
Round 9: ssk, k1, c3o1l, k9, c3o1r, k1, k2tog
Round 10: k19
Round 11: ssk, k1, c3o1l, k2, yo, sk2p, yo, k2, c3o1r, k1, k2tog
Round 12: k17
Round 13: ssk, k1, c3o1l, k5, c3o1r, k1, k2tog
Round 14: ssk, k13, k2tog
Round 15: ssk, k1, 2/1lc, k3, 2/1rc, k1, k2tog
Round 16: ssk, k9, k2tog
Round 17: ssk, k1, 1/1lc, k1, 1/1rc, k1, k2tog
Round 18: ssk, k5, k2tog

Kitchener stitch the remaining stitches together. Weave in ends and block.

Heel Chart

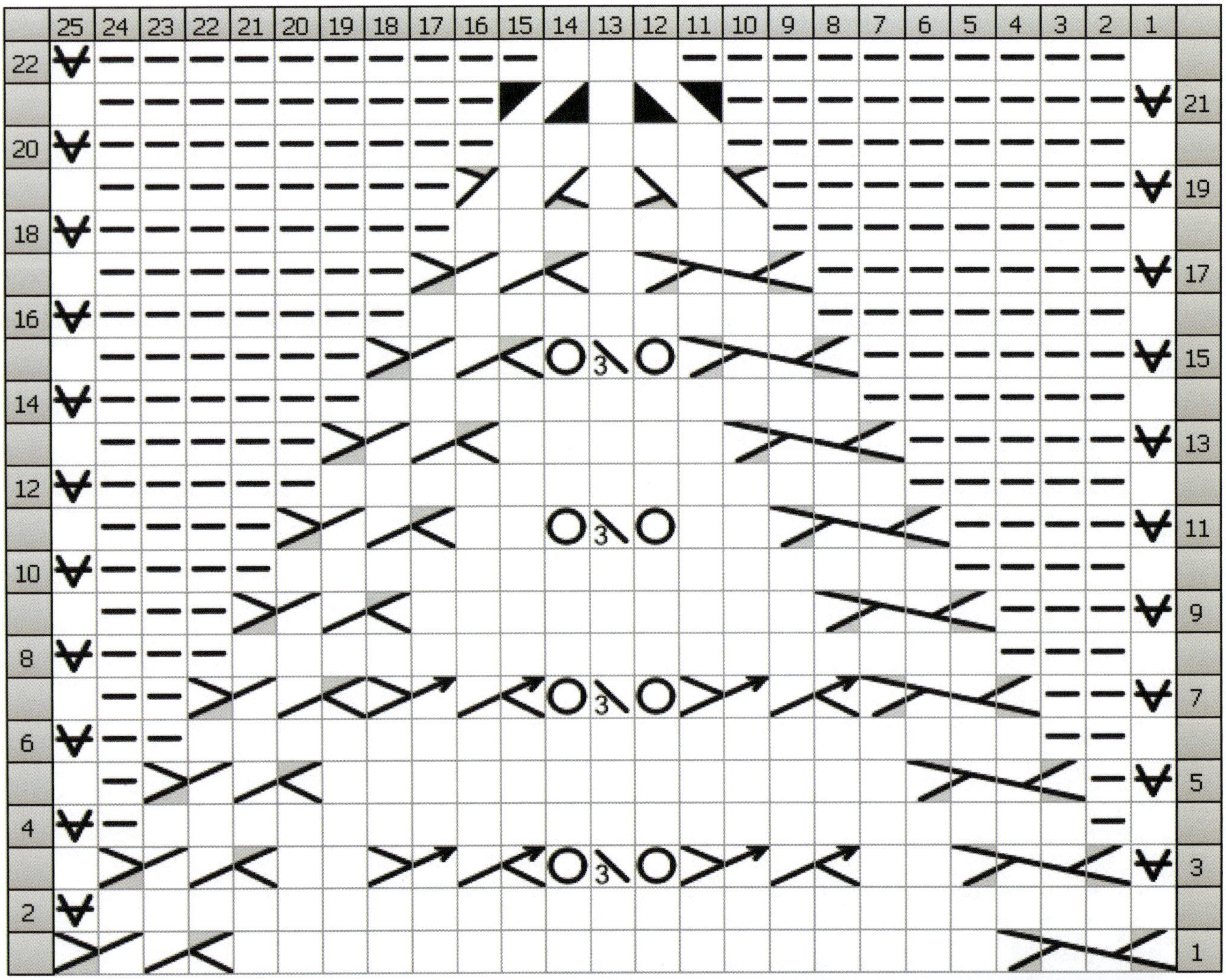

Leg Pattern Chart

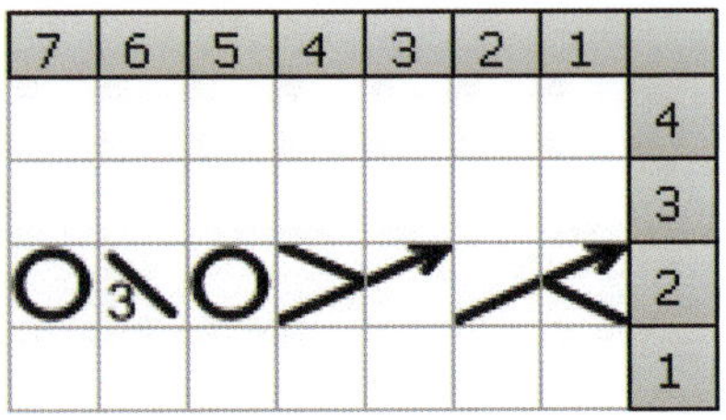

Hoppy Feet ~ A Year of Socks

Key			
⬚	1/1 Left Cross 1llc (RS) Sl 1 to front, k1, k st from cn	⬚	Knit k (RS) Knit
⬚	1/1 Right Cross 1lrc (RS) Sl 1 to back, k1, k st from cn	/	Knit 2 Together k2tog (RS) Knit 2 stitches together
⬚	2/1 Left Cross 2llc (RS) Sl 2 to front, k1, k2 from cn	—	Purl p (RS) Purl
⬚	2/1 LPC 2llpc (RS) Sl 2 to cn, hold to front, p; k2 from cn	3	SK2P sk2p (RS) Slip K2tog PSSO
⬚	2/1 Right Cross 2lrc (RS) Sl 1 to back, k2, k1 from cn	V	Slip With Yarn In Back slip wyib (RS) yarn in back
⬚	2/1 RPC 2lrpc (RS) Sl 1 to cn, hold to back, k2; p1 from cn	\	Slip Slip Knit ssk (RS) slip, slip, knit slipped sts together
⬚	2/2 RC 22rc (RS) Sl 2 to cn, hold to back, k2; k2 from cn	◢	Twist 2 Left t2l (RS) Cross 1st st in front, p1, k1
⬚	c3o1l (RS) Slip three stitches and cross in front of the fourth stitch, knit 1, knit 3 crossed stitches	◣	Twist 2 Right t2r (RS) Cross 2nd st in front, k1, p1
⬚	c3o1r (RS) Slip first stitch to back, k3 stitches, knit stitch in back	■	No Stitch x (RS) No Stitch
⬚	c3p1lc (RS) Slip three stitches and cross in front of the fourth stitch, purl 1, knit 3	O	Yarn Over yo (RS) Yarn Over
⬚	c3p1rc (RS) slip first stitch to back, knit 3 stitches, purl stitch in back		

Toe Chart

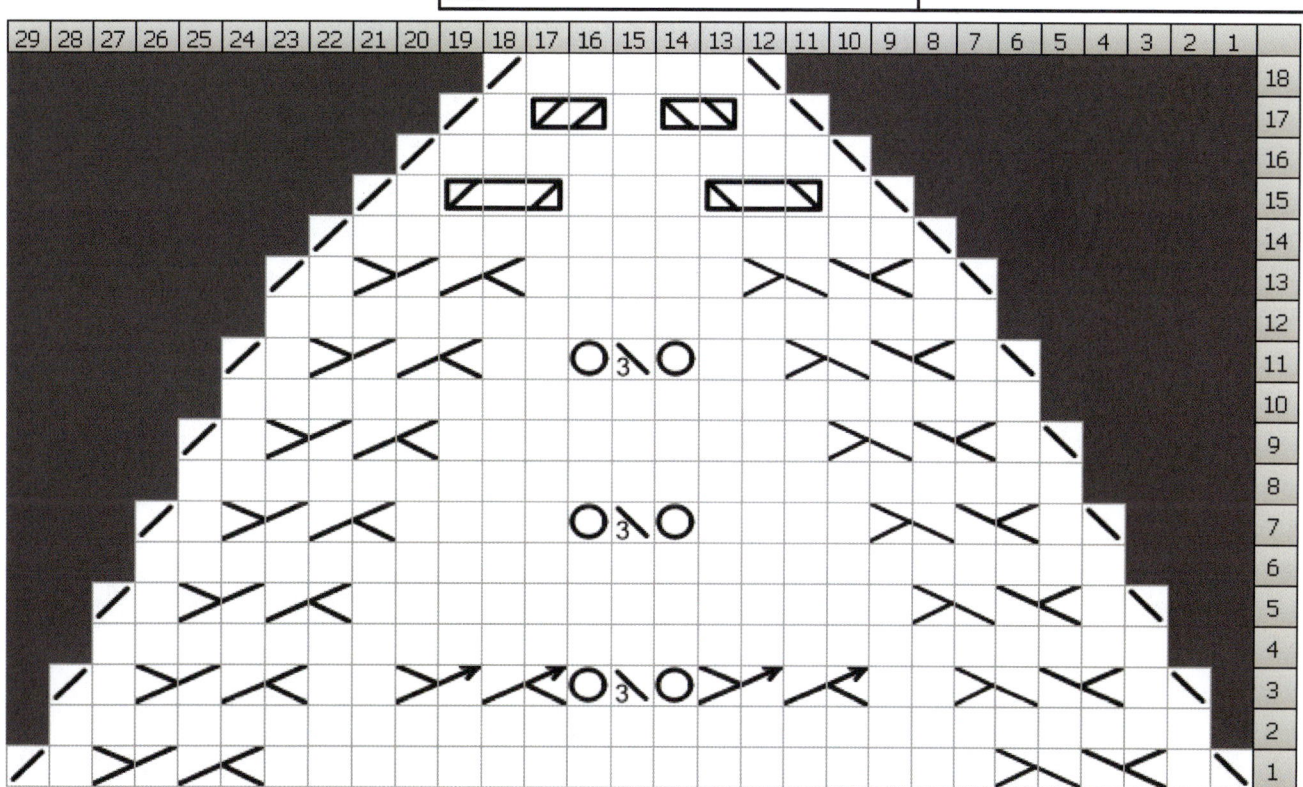

Hoarfrost Sock

11

Northern Lights Socks

February's Pattern: Northern Lights Socks

This month we are focusing on some different techniques. As the sock will have stacked ribbing, we are beginning with an Alternating Cable Cast-On. This cast-on allows us to use both knits and purls to build our cast-on. By using both knits and purls, we begin our sock in the same pattern that we will use in the cuff.

This kind of cast-on combined with a ribbed cuff causes the cast-on to "disappear" into the edge of the sock. It is a stretchy cast-on and blends into the ribbing.

The stacked ribbed cuff is achieved by knitting the ribbing in its reverse and then in the intended pattern. This creates a distinct "bend" at the point where the cuff is to be folded down. The ribs will stack inside each other creating a more compact cuff and slick appearance.

Instead of a traditional slipped stitch round heel, I chose a reverse slipped stitch round heel. The construction of this heel results in a "float" of yarn carried to the front of the work instead of the back.

Waffle ribs are a great way to break up a traditional rib pattern while still maintaining the extra stretch and fitted appearance of ribbing.
The waffle rib lends a bit of interest and helps to highlight the color changes found in the yarn. It is the resemblance of this yarn to the Northern Lights that resulted in the name.

Finally, as we approach the toe, we shift to a 3-pointed toe. The 3-pointed toe is rarely used, but lends a certain interest to the toe. It also allows us to practice stacked knit 2 togethers and slip, slip, knits to achieve strong diagonal lines in the toe.

Techniques

Alternating Cable Cast-On
Reverse Slip Stitch Patterned Heel
3-Pointed Toe
Stacked Ribbing

Skill level: This pattern is meant for an adventurous novice to intermediate knitter. Please read the entire pattern before beginning.

Yarn: 1 skein Misti Alpaca, Hand Paint Sock Yarn Fingering, 50% Alpaca, 30% Merino, 10% Silk, 10% Nylon, 437 yards, Royal Blue HS47
Needle: US 1 (2.25 mm) Hiya Hiya Steel Double Pointed Needles (DPNs) or needles to obtain gauge

Gauge: 8 stitches per inch (spi) and 9 rows per inch (rpi) OR 32 stitches & 36 rows to 4 inches/10 cm in stockinette

Size: To fit a US women's 8.5-9 shoe, approx. 8.25" circumference and 9" foot

To alter the size: Adjust your gauge to increase or decrease the circumference of the foot as needed.

Abbreviations: See the back of the book.

Northern Lights Sock

To Begin Socks:
Using the Alternating Cable Cast-on, cast-on 60 stitches in P1, K2, P1 ribbing. Join in the round, being careful not to twist. You may want to mark the beginning of your round with a stitch marker, bit of floss, or waste yarn.

Sock Cuff:
Row 1: *P1, K2, P1, repeat from * until end of round. Repeat row 1 until the cuff measures 2 inches in length.

Now you will change the direction of the ribbing so that the ribbed cuff will stack inside the rest of the cuff.

Row 1: *K1, P2, K1, repeat from * until end of round. Repeat row 1 until the cuff measures 4 total inches in length.

Heel Flap:
The heel is worked over the first 28 stitches of the row. Hold the remaining 32 stitches for the top of the foot.

Start Slipped Stitch Round Heel Flap:
Row 1: *Slip 1 purlwise with yarn in front, k1, repeat from * to end of heel flap row
Row 2: Slip 1 purlwise with yarn in back, purl to end

Repeat rows 1 and 2 of the heel flap until the heel flap measures 2 inches.

Heel Turn:
Row 1: S1, K13, SSK, K1, turn work.
Row 2: S1, P1, P2tog, P1, turn work
Row 3: S1, Knit to one stitch before gap, SSK, K1, turn work.
Row 4: S1, Purl to one stitch before gap, P2tog, P1, turn work.
Repeat rows 3 & 4 until all of the stitches have been worked. On the last 2 rows, you will not have enough stitches to knit or purl the last stitch. Knit across row. There will be 14 stitches left.

Gusset:
Pick up and knit 14 stitches along heel flap, pm, work row 1 of the foot pattern repeat 8 times, pm, then pick-up and knit 14 stitches along the other side of the heel flap. Knit 7 stitches of heel turn, PM. This is now the beginning of the row.

On the next row, K18, K2tog, K1 SM, work row 2 of foot pattern 8 times across top of foot, SM, K1, SSK, K18. On the next row, work pattern as established.

Foot Pattern repeat:
Row 1: * p4, repeat from * to end of row
Row 2-4: *k1, p2, k1, repeat from * to end of row

Continue gusset decreases:
Row A: Knit to 3 stitches before marker, K2tog, K1, SM, continue in leg pattern as established, SM, K1, SSK, knit to beginning of round marker.
Row B: Knit in pattern as established.

Repeat rows A & B until there are 60 stitches left.

Foot:
Continue knitting in established pattern until the foot measures 2 inches less than the total length of the foot (approx. 7 inches) or to desired length. Slip all markers (if used) as you come to them. End with row 4 of the leg pattern.

Toe:
Redistribute the stitches so that there are 20 stitches in each section. Use stitchmarkers if needed.

Row A: *SSK, knit to 2 stitches before stitchmarker/end of needle K2tog, repeat from * 2 more times
Row B: Knit all stitches

Repeat rows A & B 10 total times. Then repeat row A 4 more times.

Cut yarn and run through the remaining 6 stitches. Weave in ends and block.

February's Pattern: Northern Lights Mitts

With so much yarn left after knitting my Northern Lights Socks, I decided the very thing we needed was a pair of mitts to match. So, I whipped out this pair of waffle rib patterned mitts. This pattern used only part of the remaining ball, making it a very quick and economical knit!

Skill Level: This pattern is meant for an adventurous intermediate to advanced knitter. Please read the entire pattern before beginning.

Yarn: 1 skein Misti Alpaca, Hand Paint Sock Yarn Fingering, 50% Alpaca, 30% Merino, 10% Silk, 10% Nylon, 437 yards, Royal Blue HS47 (1/3 skein needed, approx. 150 yards)

Needle: US 1 (2.25 mm) Signature Steel Double Pointed Needles (DPNs) or needles to obtain gauge

Gauge: 8 stitches per inch (spi) and 9 rows per inch (rpi) OR 32 stitches & 36 rows to 4 inches/10 cm in stockinette

Size: To fit a US women's medium wrist, approx. 7.5" circumference

To alter the size: Adjust your gauge to increase or decrease the circumference of the mitt as needed.

Abbreviations: See the back of the book.

Northern Lights Mitts

To Begin Mitts:
Cast on 52 stitches. Join in the round, being careful not to twist. You may want to mark the beginning of your round with a stitch marker, bit of floss, or waste yarn.

Wrist:
Following row 1 of the waffle rib pattern repeat, establish ribbing pattern. Continue following the waffle rib pattern until the wrist measures 4 inches.

Waffle Rib Pattern:
Row 1-3: *k1, p2, k1, repeat from * to end of row
Row 4: * p4, repeat from * to end of row

Thumb Gusset:
On the next round, make 1 stitch at the beginning of the round and knit the rest of the round in established pattern.

On the next row, place marker (pm), knit 1, pm, and then work the pattern as established.

On next row: sm, M1R, k1, M1L in purl, knit rest of round as established.

On following row: sm, p3, sm, knit rest of round as established.

Continue adding stitches every other round in manner below while establishing waffle rib pattern in thumb gusset.

Row A: sm, M1R in either knit or purl as needed, knit to second marker, M1L in either knit or purl as needed, sm, continue working pattern as established.

Row B: Sm, knit in established pattern to second marker, sm, continue working pattern as established.

Repeat gusset increases 8 more times (19 stitches between markers). Remove the markers and slip the 19 stitches of the thumb gusset to a piece of dental floss or cotton yarn to hold them. Cast on 1 stitch over the gap (53 stitches) and work the rest of the round as established. On the next row, decrease the stitch just cast on by knit two together (k2tog) or purl two together (p2tog) as appropriate (52 stitches).

Resume knitting waffle rib pattern as established until the mitt measures 8 total inches or until the knitting reaches the first knuckle of your finger. End on Row 2 of the waffle rib pattern. Bind off in pattern.

Thumb:
Slip the 19 reserved stitches from the dental floss or waste yarn onto needles. Pick up 2 stitches in pattern in the gap where the gusset meets the top of the mitt and knit around the row in the pattern as established (21 total stitches). On the next row, decrease 1 of the picked up stitches to properly establish the waffle rib pattern in the thumb (20 stitches).

Knit in waffle rib pattern as established until the thumb measures 1 1/4 inches or to desired length. End with row 2 of the waffle rib pattern. Bind off in pattern.

Repeat for second mitt.

Wash and block as desired.

Dreaming of the Caribbean Socks

March's Pattern: Dreaming of the Caribbean Socks

March starts our exploration of the toe-up sock. We have tried two top-down socks already, so now it is time to try something different. Toe-up socks are always started with an invisible cast-on. There are 3 main invisible cast-ons used for toe-up socks: Judy's Magic Cast-On, the Turkish Cast-On, and the Figure Eight Cast-On.

This month I chose Judy's Magic Cast-On to start our toe-up socks. As you cast-on, be sure to pull your stitches tight to ensure an even toe. Once you have cast-on, you will start to increase your toe.

I chose an increased wedge toe with matching increases on the sides of the sock. When working your make one increases, make sure you keep your picked-up yarn tight for a seamless increase. As you transition into the foot, the sole stitches are kept in stockinette while the top of the foot stitches are patterned.

Slipped stitches are commonly used in heel flaps to add strength, but I have chosen to highlight them as a pattern all on their own. The slipped stitches act to break up the stripe pattern in the yarn and give a sense of ribbing without having ribbing in the sock.

As we move into the heel, I have chosen a Short Row Heel for the heel turn. When working the wrap it is important to pull the wrap tight. When working the second half of the heel, knit the stitch and wraps together through the back loop.

We return to the slipped stitches for the leg, and then bloom into a scalloped cuff. The scalloped cuff is worked with yarnovers and decreases.

To ensure that our scalloped cuff has enough stretch in the bind-off, I chose Jenny's Surprisingly Stretchy Bind-Off.

Techniques

Judy's Magic Cast-On
Short Row Heel
Increased Wedge Toe
Scalloped Cuff
Jenny's Surprisingly Stretchy Cast-Off

Skill Level: This pattern is meant for an adventurous novice to intermediate knitter. Please read the entire pattern before beginning.

Yarn: 2 skeins Blue Ridge Yarns, Tango, 100% Superwash Merino Wool, 400 yards, Caribbean Cooler (034)

Needle: US 2 (2.75 mm) & 3 (3.25 mm) Hiya Hiya Steel Double Pointed Needles (DPNs) or needles to obtain gauge

Gauge: 6 stitches per inch (spi) and 9 rows per inch (rpi) OR 24 stitches & 36 rows to 4 inches/10 cm in stockinette on US 2

Size: To fit a US women's 8.5-9 shoe, approx. 8.25" circumference and 9" foot

To alter the size: Adjust your gauge to increase or decrease the circumference of the foot as needed.

Abbreviations: See the back of the book.

To Begin Socks:
Using Judy's Magic Cast-on, cast-on 12 stitches. You may want to mark the beginning of your round with a stitch marker, bit of floss, or waste yarn.

Toe:
Knit 2 rows plain. Use stitchmarkers to mark 2 sections of 6 stitches each.

Row A: *K1, M1L, knit to one stitch before end of section, M1R, K1, repeat from * one more time (4 stitches increased)
Row B: Knit all stitches

Repeat rows A & B 9 total times. You should have 48 total stitches.

Foot:
The foot is now divided into 2 sections. The first 24 stitches are the sole of the foot and the last 24 stitches are the top of the foot.

Foot Pattern:
Row A: Knit to 1st stitchmarker (sole stitches),sm,* K1, S1 purlwise, repeat from * across row to stitchmarker
Row B: Knit all stitches

Continue knitting rows A & B until the foot measures 2 inches less than the total length of the foot (approx. 7 inches) or to desired length. Slip all markers (if used) as you come to them. End with row B of the foot pattern.

Short Row Heel:
The heel is worked over the first 24 stitches of the row. Hold the remaining 24 stitches for the top of the foot.

Heel Expansion:
Row 1: Knit to 1 stitch before marker, move yarn to front and wrap the yarn around the last stitch, turn work.
Row 2: Purl to 1 stitch before marker, move yarn to back and wrap yarn aroudn the last stitch, turn work
Row 3: Knit to one stitch before gap, wrap & turn
Row 4: Purl to one stitch before gap, wrap and turn.

Repeat rows 3 & 4 until 8 stitches remain unworked in the center of the heel.

Heel Reduction:
Row 1: Knit to one stitch before gap, knit that stitch together with the wrap, wrap & turn the next stitch
Row 2: Purl to one stitch before gap, purl that stitch together with the wrap, wrap and turn the next stitch.

Repeat rows 1 & 2 until all of the stitches have been worked.

Leg:
Begin working in the round once more by establishing the leg pattern.

Leg Pattern:
Row A: * K1, S1 purlwise, repeat from * to end of row
Row B: Knit all stitches

Repeat Rows A & B for 1 inch, switch to larger (US 3) needles. Repeat rows A & B until leg measures 7 inches, or to desired length.

Sock Cuff:
Round 1: *yo, k1, sk2p, k1, yo, k1, repeat from * across round
Round 2: knit all stitches

Repeat rounds 1 & 2 five total times. Bind off using Jenny's Surprisingly Stretchy Bind-Off. Weave in ends and block.

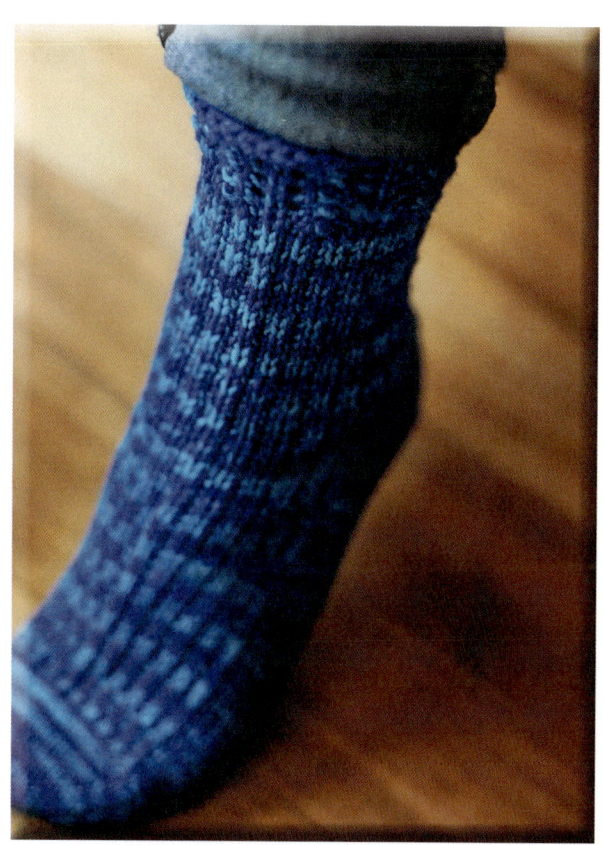

Bouncing Bunnies Socks

April's Pattern: Bouncing Bunnies Socks

Our journey with the Bouncing Bunnies Socks begins with a 2-Color Braided Cast-on. You will follow the colors on row 1 of the cuff chart to cast-on. First you will have a purple stitch, then 6 white stitches, then a purple stitch. It is important to remember to keep twisting the color toward you as you switch from purple to white and back again.

We then progress to colorwork ribbing. It is important to remember throughout the sock to keep your floats soft and open. Do not tighten your stitches too much or you will be unable to pull the sock over your heel. We work K1P1 ribbing in a charted wave pattern. On three rows, we will work with all 3 colors used in the pattern. These are the only 3 rows which require all 3 yarns.

Once the ribbing is complete we will move to some plain stockinette for a few rows before beginning the leg pattern. It is a good idea to continue to check your floats every few stitches and to try pulling the sock over your foot after working 5-9 rows of the leg chart. Colorwork can easily tighten if your floats are not soft and open.

Once through the leg chart, it is easy stockinette down to the heel. The heel is a colorwork patterned heel, but a traditional heel flap. Once the heel flap has been worked, you will turn the heel, pick up the gusset stitches by knitting under both strands of the slipped stitches, and reurning to plain stockinette.

The foot is worked until 2.5 inches from the desired length of your toe. Then you will begin the colorwork toe chart. As you work towards the decreases, you will start with staggered decreases and then move into every round decreases to finish the toe. It is important to pull your decreases tight to prevent "drifting" between the colorwork sections.

Techniques

2-Color Braided Cast-On
Colorwork Patterned Heel Flap
Colorwork Patterned Wedge Toe
Colorwork

Skill Level: This pattern is meant for an adventurous novice to intermediate knitter. Please read the entire pattern before beginning.

Yarn: 1 skein Cascade Heritage Silk, 437 yards, 85% Superwash Merino, 15% Mulberry Silk, 1 skein Madelinetosh Unicorn Tails in Fathom and 1 skein in Flashdance, 52 yards, 100% Superwash

Needle: US 1 (2.25 mm) Signature Steel Double Pointed Needles (DPNs) or needles to obtain gauge

Gauge: 8.5 stitches per inch (spi) and 10 rows per inch (rpi) OR 34 stitches & 40 rows to 4 inches/10 cm in stockinette

Size: To fit a US women's 8.5-9 shoe, approx. 8.25" circumference and 9" foot

To alter the size: Adjust your gauge to increase or decrease the circumference of the foot as needed.

Abbreviations: See the back of the book.

To Begin Socks:
Using the 2-Color Cast-On and following the first row of the Cuff Chart, cast-on 64 stitches. Join in the round, being careful not to twist. You may want to mark the beginning of your round with a stitch marker, bit of floss, or waste yarn.

Sock Cuff:
Starting with row 2 and following the Cuff Chart for color, work 1 x 1 ribbing (K1, P1) for the cuff. For example, the first row would be: *purple (K1), white (P1, K1,)x2, K1, purple, (P1,) repeat from * 8 total times.

Continue knitting in ribbing pattern and following the color chart through row 17.

Leg:
The leg is now divided into 2 sections. The first 32 stitches are the back of the leg and the last 32 stitches are the front of the leg. Continue knitting down the leg in stockinette.

Knit 5 rows of white. Then start the Leg Chart. Repeat the sock leg chart twice for each row (once for the front and once for the back). Continue to knit the leg in color pattern from rows 1-18.

Then continue knitting the leg in white until the leg measures 7 inches from cast-on edge or to desired length. Slip all markers as you come to them, if used.

Heel:
The heel is worked over the first 32 stitches of the row. Hold the remaining 32 stitches for the top of the foot. Work the heel flat per the Heel Chart. Slip the first stitch of each row.

Heel Turn:
Row 1: S1, K16, SSK, K1, turn work.
Row 2: S1, P3, P2tog, P1, turn work
Row 3: S1, Knit to one stitch before gap, SSK, K1, turn work.
Row 4: S1, Purl to one stitch before gap, P2tog, P1, turn work.

Repeat rows 3 & 4 until all of the stitches have been worked. Knit across row. There will be 18 stitches left.

Gusset:
Pick-up and knit 12 stitches along heel flap, pm, knit across 32 stitches for top of foot, pm, then pick-up and knit 12 stitches along the other side of the heel flap. To pick up, work the new stitch under both strands of each slipped stitch along the edge in order to keep the edge tight and clean. Knit 9 stitches of heel turn, PM. This is now the beginning of the row.

Gusset decreases:
Row A: Knit to 3 stitches before marker, K2tog, K1, SM, continue in leg pattern as established, SM, K1, SSK, knit to beginning of round marker.
Row B: Knit in pattern as established.

Repeat rows A & B until there are 64 stitches left.

Foot:
Continue working the foot by knitting every stitch in white until foot measures 6.5 inches from heel or to desired length. Stop your foot 2.5 inches from your total desired length.

Toe:
Remove beginning of round marker. Knit 16 stitches. Place beginning of round marker. Begin toe chart. You will knit the toe chart twice for each row.

Kitchener stitch the last 16 stitches together. Weave in ends and block.

Leg Chart

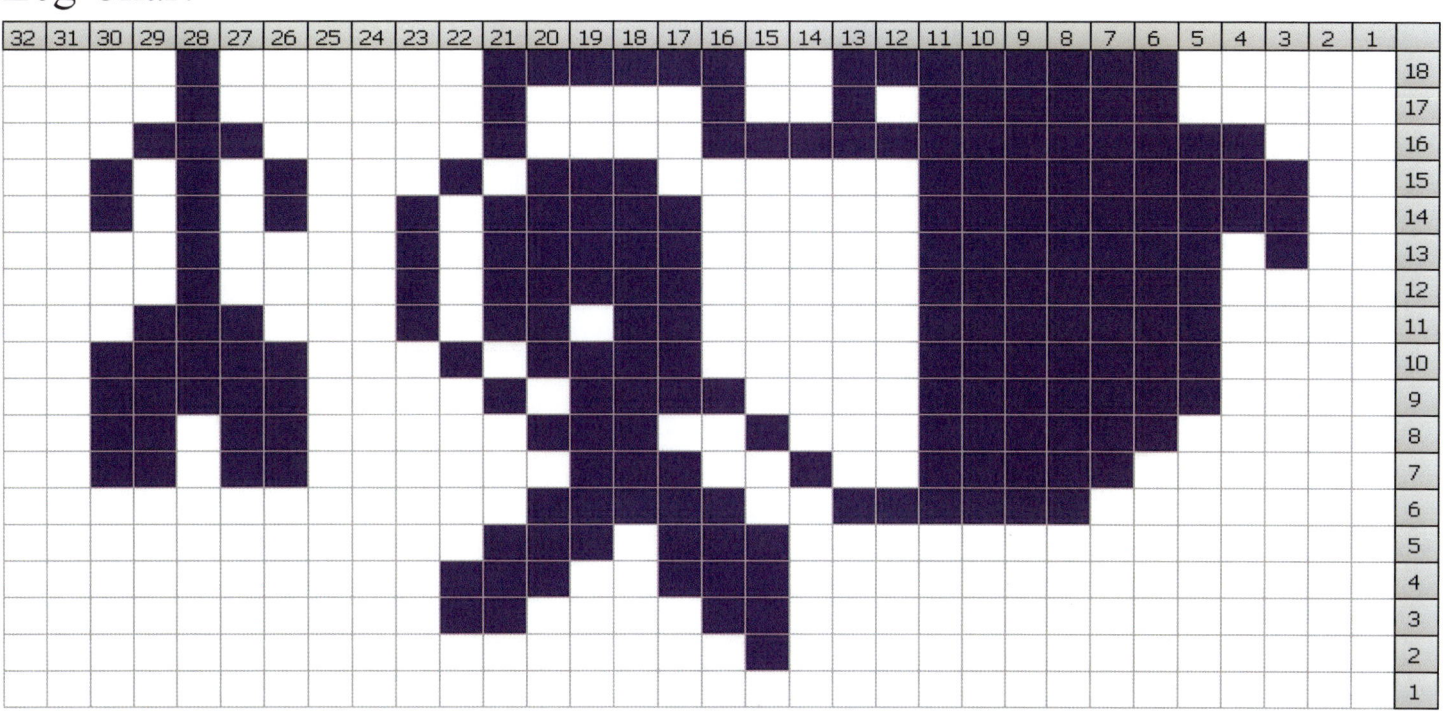

As this pair of socks is worked from the cuff to the toe, the charts will appear to be upside down. Like magic, the rabbit will appear right-side-up when the sock is worn.

Toe Chart

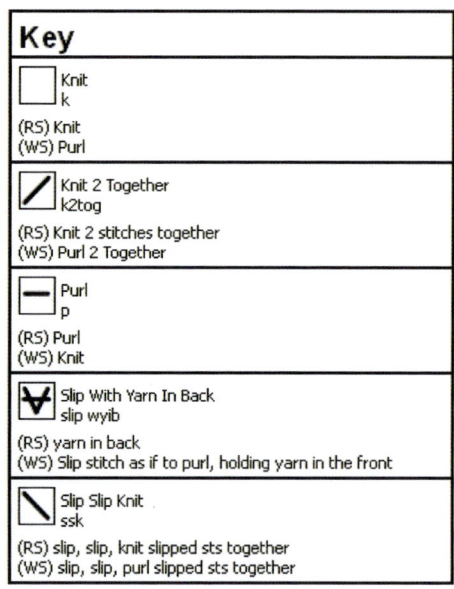

Heel Chart

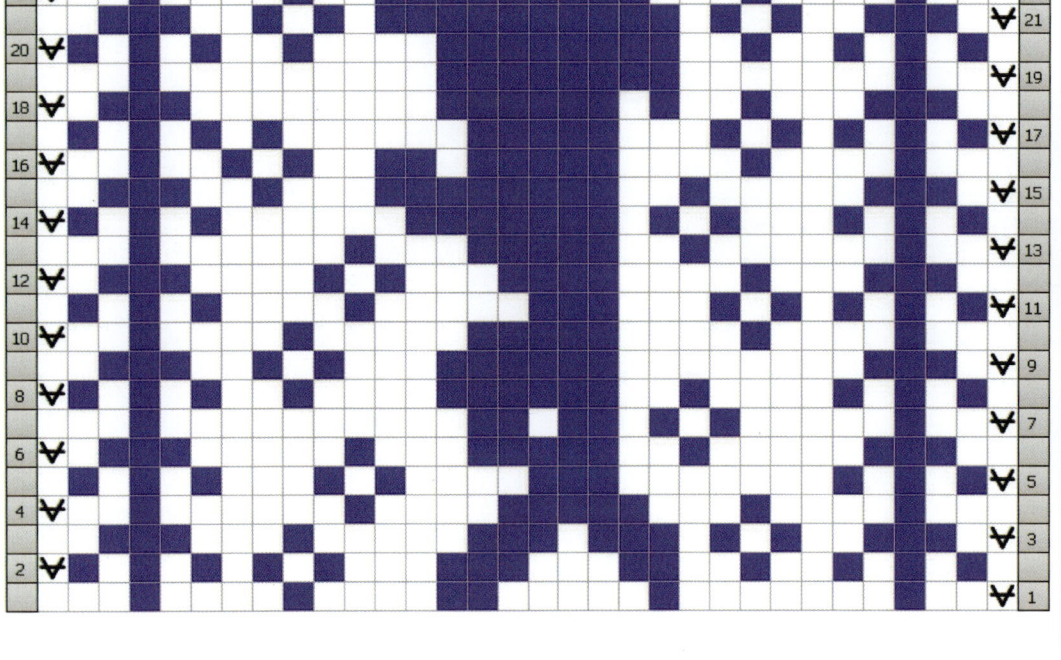

Cuff Chart

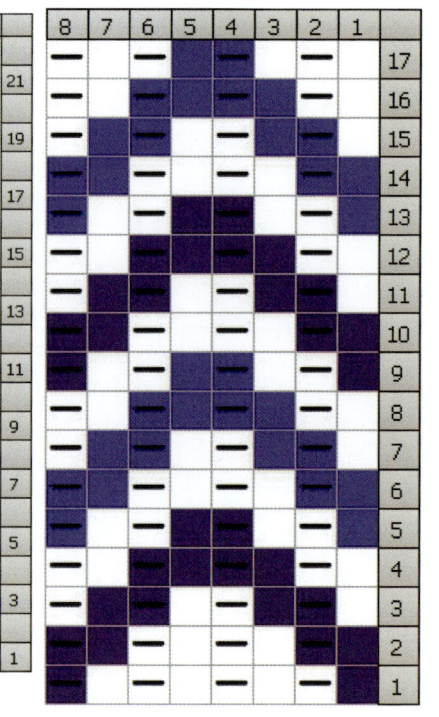

Pushing Up Tulips Socks

May's Pattern: Pushing Up Tulips Socks

May continues our exploration of the toe-up sock. We tried one toe-up sock earlier in the year, so now it is time to try another one. The Turkish Cast-On can be tricky. Make sure that you knit into the front of the stich as you knit the stitches on the first needle and into the back of the stitch on the second needle.

You will transition from the Turkish Cast-On into an increased 4-point toe. This is accomplished through make one left increases. The increases are stacked and create a lovely petal effect as you knit the sock.

We build the flower effect further with the twisted stitch tulip cables that extend up the sock.

In this sock, we use a Toe-Up Round Heel which requires that we reverse the process of a Top-Down Round Heel. First, we will add stitches in the gusset expansion. Next, the heel is turned using short rows. Then the heel flap is knit and attached to the stitches added during the gusset expansion. The sock is then knit in the round up the leg once more.

Finally, the hem is a picot hem. It is not a Picot Cast-Off, but a turned Picot Hem. First a few rounds are knit plain. Next a row of yarnovers is knit. Finally a few more rows of plain knitting are added. When the hem is folded down and hemmed into place, a row of "picots" appears on the top of the sock.

Some things to remember:
~Work each heel in its entirety before moving to the other sock.
~Bind off the sock loosely so that it does not bind your leg when it is sewn down.

Techniques

Turkish Cast-On
Toe-Up Round Heel
Increased 4-Point Toe
Twisted Stitch Cables
Picot Hem Bind-Off

Skill level: This pattern is meant for an adventurous novice to intermediate knitter. Please read the entire pattern before beginning.

Yarn: 1 skein Black Trillium Lilt 85% Superwash Merino Wool, 15% Mulberry Silk, 405 yards, Lemon Chiffon

Needle: US 1 (2.25 mm) Hiya Hiya Steel Double Pointed Needles (DPNs) or needles to obtain gauge

Gauge: 8 stitches per inch (spi) and 9 rows per inch (rpi) OR 32 stitches & 36 rows to 4 inches/10 cm in stockinette on US 2

Size: To fit a US women's 8.5-9 shoe, approx. 8.25" circumference and 9" foot

To alter the size: Adjust your gauge to increase or decrease the circumference of the foot as needed.

Abbreviations: See the back of the book.

To Begin Socks:
Using a Turkish Cast-on, cast-on 16 stitches. You may want to mark the beginning of your round with a stitch marker, bit of floss, or waste yarn.

Toe:
Knit 1 row plain. Use stitchmarkers to mark 4 sections of 4 stitches each.

Row A: *K1, M1L, knit to end of section, SM, repeat from * three more times (4 stitches increased)
Row B: Knit all stitches

Repeat rows A & B 11 total times. You should have 60 total stitches.

Foot:
Rearrange your stitchmarkers so that the foot is divided into 2 sections. The first 30 stitches are the top of the foot and the last 30 stitches are the sole of the foot.

Foot Pattern:
Row A: Knit Tulip Pattern row 1, knit 10, knit tulip pattern row 1, sm, knit to end of row
Row B: Knit next Tulip Pattern row, knit 10, knit next tulip pattern row, sm, knit to end of row

The Tulip Pattern repeats from rows 3 through 21.

Continue knitting pattern as established, following the pattern repeat, until the foot measures 3 1/2 inches less than the total length of the foot (approx. 5 1/2 inches) or to desired length. Slip all markers (if used) as you come to them. The Tulip Pattern Repeat is charted later in the pattern for those who prefer charts. A blue line demarcates the set-up rows from the pattern repeat.

Tulip Pattern:

Setup Rows:
Row1: p4, k1 tbl2, p4
Row 2: p4, 1lrc, p4

Repeat Rows:
Row 3: p3, 1lrc, 1llc, p3
Row 4: p2, t2r, k1 tbl2, t2l, p2
Row 5: p2, k1 tbl, p1, k1 tbl2, p1, k1 tbl, p2
Row 6: p2, k1 tbl, p1, k1 tbl2, p1, k1 tbl, p2
Row 7: p2, k1 tbl, p1, k1 tbl2, p1, k1 tbl, p2
Row 8: p2, k1 tbl, p1, k1 tbl2, p1, k1 tbl, p2
Row 9: p2, k1 tbl, p1, k1 tbl2, p1, k1 tbl, p2
Row 10: p2, k1 tbl, p1, k1 tbl2, p1, k1 tbl, p2
Row 11: p1, t2r, p1, 1lrc, p1, t2l, p1
Row 12: t2r, p2, k1 tbl2, p2, t2l
Row 13: k1 tbl, p3, 1lrc, p3, k1 tbl
Row 14: k1 tbl, p2, t2r, t2l, p2, k1 tbl
Row 15: p2, 1lrc, p2, 1llc, p2
Row 16: p1, t2r, t2l, t2r, t2l, p1
Row 17: p1, k1 tbl, p2, 1lrc, p2, k1 tbl, p1
Row 18: p1, t2l, t2r, t2l, t2r, p1
Row 19: p2, 1llc, k2, 1lrc, p2
Row 20: p3, t2l, t2r, p3
Row 21: p4, 1lrc, p4

Gusset Expansion:
Row A Top: Knit next row of tulip pattern repeat, knit 10 stitches, knit next row of tulip pattern repeat, M1L, knit to end of round, M1R.
Row B: Knit next row of tulip pattern repeat, knit 10 stitches, knit next row of tulip pattern repeat, knit across all sole stitches.

Continue to knit rows A & B of the gusset expansion until the sock measures 9 inches (or to desired length). You should have 90 stitches.

Heel Turn:
Knit across the top of the foot (first 30 stitches). Note the tulip pattern row on which you ended_____.
Slip marker, knit 15 stitches, place marker. If knitting socks 2-at-a-time, work 1 heel turn and flap at a time.

The heel is worked over the middle 30 stitches of the sole. 30 stitches are held for the top of the foot, 15 stitches on each side of the sole are held to be knit during the heel flap. If you are working the socks two-at-a-time, you need to work each heel in its entirety.

Row 1: K29, wrap & turn (w & t) next stitch, pm.
Row 2: Purl to 1 stitch before marker, w & t.
Row 3: Knit to 2 stitches before wrapped stitch, w & t.
Row 4: Purl to 2 stitches before wrapped stitch, w & t.

Repeat rows 3 and 4 until four stitches remain unwrapped.

Slip the first stitch, then knit across the heel; as you come to the wrapped stitches, pick up the wrap and knit it together with the stitch it is wrapping through the back loop (k2togtbl) until all but one stitch has been worked before the marker. Knit together the last stitch, wrap, and the stitch following the stitchmarker that was reserved for the heel flap (k3tog). You have now decreased 1 of the gusset stitches.

Pushing Up Tulips Sock

Slip the first stitch, then purl back across the heel; as you come to the wrapped stitches, pick up the wrap and purl it together with the stitch it is wrapping (p2tog) until all but one stitch has been worked before the marker. Purl together the last stitch, wrap, and the stitch following the stitchmarker that was reserved for the heel flap (p3tog). You have now decreased 1 of the gusset stitches.

Heel Flap:
Row A: *S1, K1, repeat from * until end of row, remembering to work the last stitch as a k2tog with 1 stitch from the gusset stitches.
Row B: S1, purl across row, remembering to work the last stitch as a p2tog with 1 stitch from the gusset stitches.

Repeat Rows A & B until all of the gusset stitches have been decreased. You should have 30 sole stitches and 30 foot pattern stitches left (60 total stitches).

Leg:
Begin working in the round once more by knitting the next row of the Tulip Pattern repeat, knitting 10 stitches, knitting the next row of the Tulip Pattern repeat, and knitting across the back leg stitches. (60 total stitches).

Continue knitting the leg in the established pattern until the leg measures 8 inches or to desired length. End the pattern on row 21 before starting cuff.

Sock Cuff:
Rows 1-3: Knit
Row 4: *K2tog, YO, repeat from * to end of row.
Rows 5-7: Knit

Bind off using the traditional bind off. Hem row 7 to row 1 on the inside, but do not pull tight. Weave in ends and block.

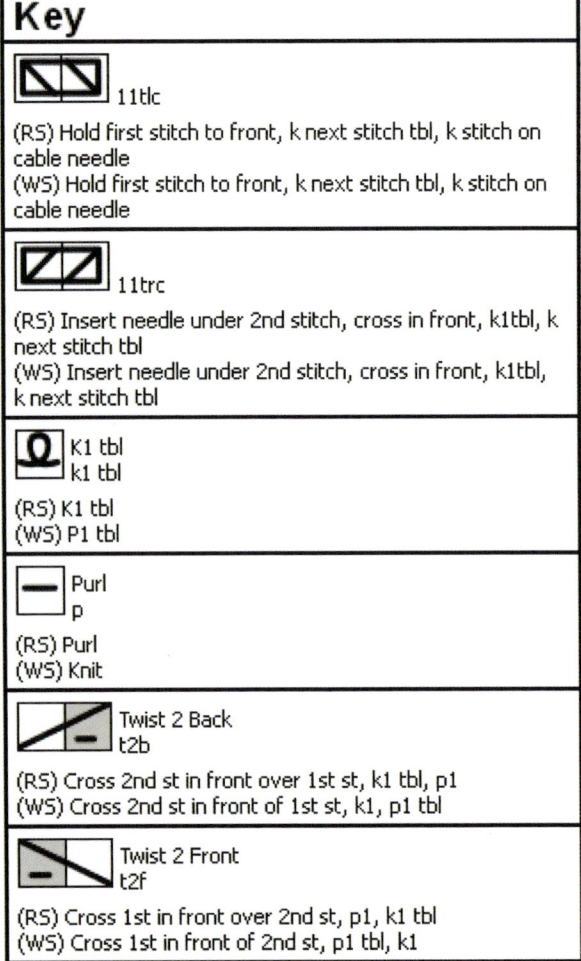

Key

- 1 1tlc
  (RS) Hold first stitch to front, k next stitch tbl, k stitch on cable needle
  (WS) Hold first stitch to front, k next stitch tbl, k stitch on cable needle

- 1 1trc
  (RS) Insert needle under 2nd stitch, cross in front, k1tbl, k next stitch tbl
  (WS) Insert needle under 2nd stitch, cross in front, k1tbl, k next stitch tbl

- K1 tbl / k1 tbl
  (RS) K1 tbl
  (WS) P1 tbl

- Purl / p
  (RS) Purl
  (WS) Knit

- Twist 2 Back / t2b
  (RS) Cross 2nd st in front over 1st st, k1 tbl, p1
  (WS) Cross 2nd st in front of 1st st, k1, p1 tbl

- Twist 2 Front / t2f
  (RS) Cross 1st in front over 2nd st, p1, k1 tbl
  (WS) Cross 1st in front of 2nd st, p1 tbl, k1

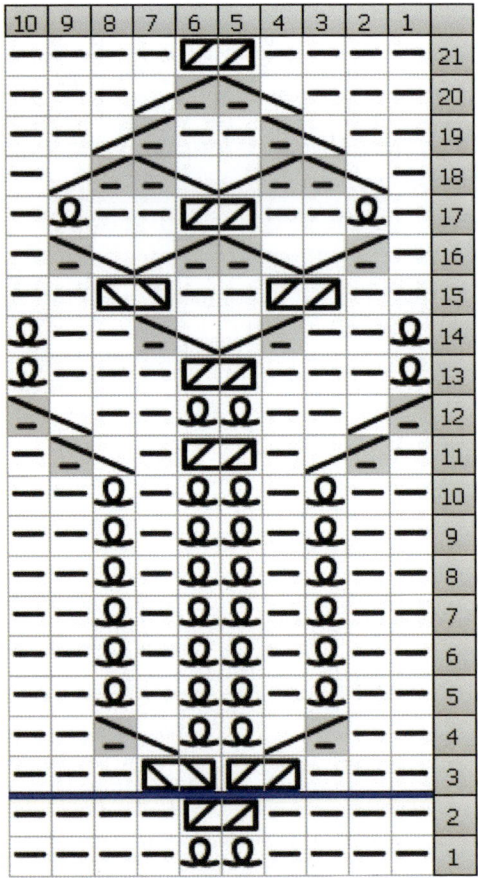

28   Hoppy Feet ~ A Year of Socks

Honeybee Socks

June's Pattern: Honeybee Socks

We begin June's Honeybee Socks with Tillybuddy's Very Stretchy Cast-On. This is a loose and innovative cast-on that can be a little tricky to start, but creates a looped edge along the top of our sock. The cuff is a rather traditional 2 x 2 ribbing which then works well with honeycomb cables and bit of lace for the honeybee wings.

I kept the honeybee wings on the leg, but chose not to carry them down the heel or foot. This makes the socks both easier and more difficult to work. Easier because you have fewer pattern stitches, but difficult because you are changing your pattern half way through!

For the heel flap, I chose to carry the honeycomb down with a purl panel on both sides. We then work the Welsh heel turn and I found it to be just tricky enough to warrant a video on turning the Welsh heel. If you follow my directions without question, it will all work out.

From there we transition into a different pattern for the foot. We retain the honeycomb cables and establish stockinette panels on the sides which helps the foot pattern to blend in with the sole stitches.

I chose to carry the honeycomb cables down the toe as well. You work a regular flat toe with decreases on the sides, but continue to work in pattern with the honeycombs, decreasing into the pattern as needed. You may not be able to cross all of the cables in a pattern row on the toe as you work your decreases. Don't worry about that, just keep working those decreases. When you reach the last few stitches, kitchener your toe together.

Techniques

Tillybuddy's Very Stretchy Cast-On
Welsh Heel
Flat Toe
Cables
Lace

Skill level: This pattern is meant for an adventurous novice to intermediate knitter. Please read the entire pattern before beginning.

Yarn: 1 skein Broken Pattern Bamboo Sock, 430 yards, 60% Merino, 30% Bamboo, 10% Nylon

Needle: US 1 (2.25 mm) Signature Steel Double Pointed Needles (DPNs) or needles to obtain gauge

Gauge: 7.25 stitches per inch (spi) and 9 rows per inch (rpi) OR 29 stitches & 36 rows to 4 inches/10 cm in stockinette

Size: To fit a US women's 8.5-9 shoe, approx. 8.5" circumference and 9" foot

To alter the size: Adjust your gauge to increase or decrease the circumference of the foot as needed.

Abbreviations: See the back of the book.

To Begin Socks:
Using Tillybuddy's Very Stretchy Cast-On, cast-on 56 stitches. You may want to mark the beginning of your round with a stitch marker, bit of floss, or waste yarn.

Sock Cuff:
Establish the sock cuff ribbing: *P1, K2, P1,* repeat from * to * around the sock. Continue in established pattern for 1 inch.

Knit 1 round, increasing 2 stitches evenly around the sock.

Leg:
The leg is now divided into 2 sections. The first 29 stitches are the back of the leg and the last 29 stitches are the front of the leg. Place markers to divide your stitches evenly from the beginning of the round.

Establish the leg pattern by following round 1 of the Leg Pattern chart (LPC) twice. The pattern chart shows you half of the stitches in the sock. Slip all markers as you come to them.

Leg Pattern Chart (Written):
Round 1: p3, k2tog, yo, k1, p2, k2, p2, k2, p2, k2, p2, k1, yo, ssk, p2
Round 2: p3, k3, p1, 1bc, 1fc, 1bc, 1fc, 1bc, 1fc, 1bc, 1fc, p1, k3, p2
Round 3: p2, k2tog, yo, k2tog, yo, p1, k1, p2, k2, p2, k2, p2, k2, p2, k1, p1, yo, ssk, yo, ssk, p1
Round 4: p2, k3, p1 tbl, p1, k1, p2, k2, p2, k2, p2, k2, p2, k1, p1, p1 tbl, k3, p1
Round 5: p1, k2tog, yo, k2tog, yo, p2, k1, p2, k2, p2, k2, p2, k2, p2, k1, p2, yo, ssk, yo, ssk
Round 6: p1, k3, p1 tbl, p2, 1fc, 1bc, 1fc, 1bc, 1fc, 1bc, 1fc, 1bc, p2, p1 tbl, k3
Round 7: p1, yo, sk2p, yo, p4, k2, p2, k2, p2, k2, p2, k2, p4, yo, sk2p, yo
Round 8: p1, p1 tbl, p1, p1 tbl, p4, k2, p2, k2, p2, k2, p4, p1 tbl, p1, p1 tbl

Continue to follow the chart as established with rounds 2 through 8. Repeat rows 1-8 until the leg measures 7 inches from cast-on edge or to desired length. Slip all markers as you come to them, if used.

Heel:
The heel is worked over the first 29 stitches of the row. Hold the remaining 29 stitches for the top of the foot. Work the heel flat per the Heel Chart. Remember to slip the first stitch of each row.

Row 1 (rs): slip wyif, p7, k2, p2, k2, p2, k2, p2, k2, p7
Row 2 (ws): slip wyib, k5, 1fc, 1bc, 1fc, 1bc, 1fc, 1bc, 1fc, 1bc, k7
Row 3 (rs): slip wyif, p6, k1, p2, k2, p2, k2, p2, k2, p2, k1, p6
Row 4 (ws): slip wyib, k5, p1, k2, p2, k2, p2, k2, p2, k2, p1, k7
Row 5 (rs): slip wyif, p6, k1, p2, k2, p2, k2, p2, k2, p2, k1, p6
Row 6 (ws): slip wyib, k5, 1bc, 1fc, 1bc, 1fc, 1bc, 1fc, 1bc, 1fc, k7
Row 7 (rs): slip wyif, p7, k2, p2, k2, p2, k2, p2, k2, p7
Row 8 (ws): slip wyib, k6, p2, k2, p2, k2, p2, k2, p2, k8

Repeat rows 1-8 until the heel measures 2 inches long or to desired length.

Heel Turn:
Row 1: S1, K3, YO, K2tog, K5, K2tog, K1, PM, K2, k2tog, k5, K2tog, turn work.
Row 2: YO, P19, turn work
Row 3: YO, K2tog, K5, K2tog, K3, k2tog, k5, K2tog, turn work.
Row 4: YO, P19, turn work.

Repeat rows 3 & 4 twice. Then knit row 3 again (5 more rows worked). There will be 18 stitches left including the YO. The marker in the middle of the heel is now the beginning of the round.

Gusset:
Pick-up and knit 11 stitches along heel flap, pm, knit row 1 of Foot Chart across top of foot, pm, then pick-up and knit 11 stitches along the other side of the heel flap, K2tog (the YO plus 1 stitch of the heel), K7.
Gusset decreases:

Row A: Knit to 3 stitches before marker, K2tog, K1, SM, continue in leg pattern as established, SM, K1, SSK, knit to beginning of round marker.
Row B: Knit in pattern as established.

Repeat rows A & B until there are 58 stitches left.

Foot:
Continue working foot by knitting pattern as established until foot measures 7 inches from heel or to desired length. Stop your foot 2 inches from your total desired length.

Foot Chart (Written):
Round 1: k5, p3, k2, p2, k2, p2, k2, p2, k2, p3, k4
Round 2: k5, p2, 1bc, 1fc, 1bc, 1fc, 1bc, 1fc, 1bc, 1fc, p2, k4

Honeybee Sock

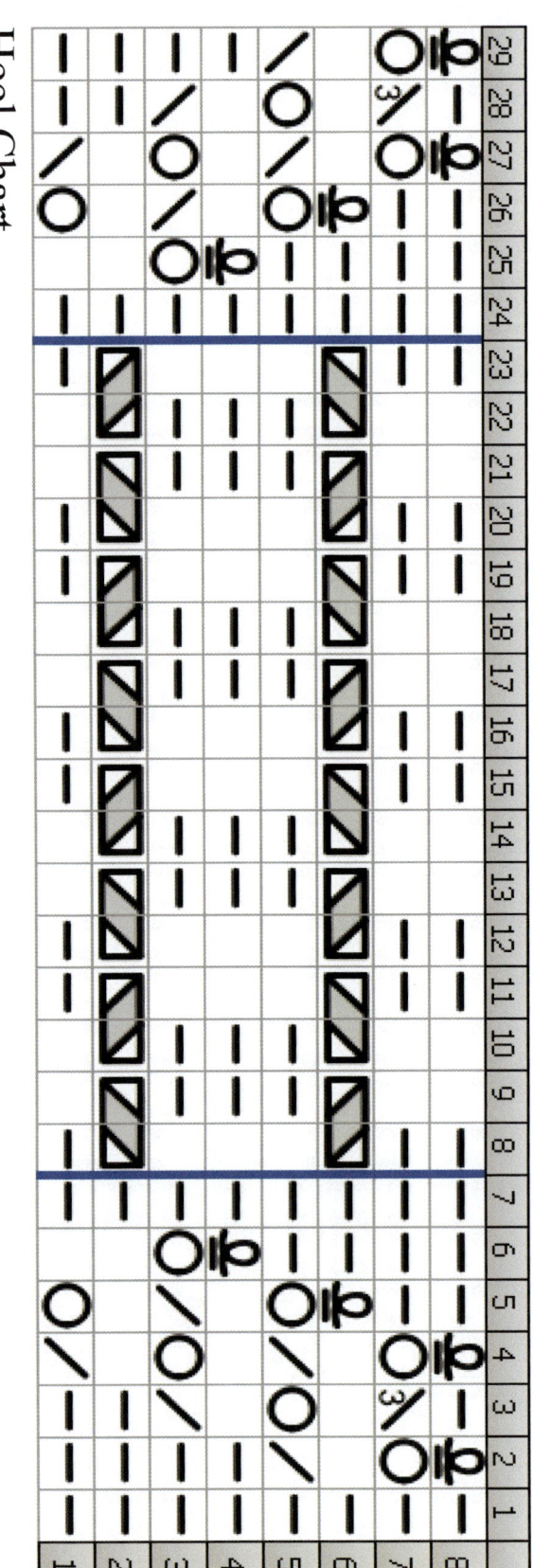

Leg Pattern Chart

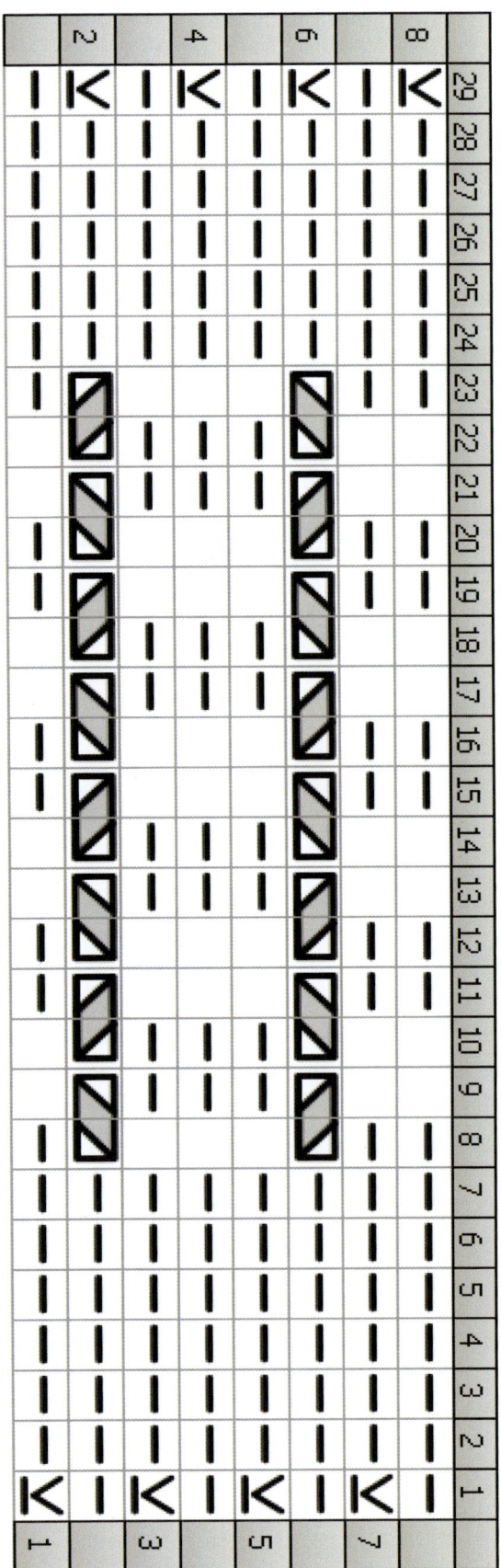

Heel Chart

The blue lines are where I place my stitchmarkers to help me remember where the cables are when I am knitting the leg.

Round 3: k5, p2, k1, p2, k2, p2, k2, p2, k2, p2, k1, p2, k4
Round 4: k5, p2, k1, p2, k2, p2, k2, p2, k2, p2, k1, p2, k4
Round 5: k5, p2, k1, p2, k2, p2, k2, p2, k2, p2, k1, p2, k4
Round 6: k5, p2, 1fc, 1bc, 1fc, 1bc, 1fc, 1bc, 1fc, 1bc, p2, k4
Round 7: k5, p3, k2, p2, k2, p2, k2, p2, k2, p3, k4
Round 8: k5, p3, k2, p2, k2, p2, k2, p2, k2, p3, k4

Toe:
Knit to the side marker. The first 29 stitches will be the top of your toe and the last 29 stitches will be the sole of your toe.

Row A: *K1, SSK, knit in pattern to 3 stitches before stitchmarker/end of needle K2tog, K1, repeat from * 1 more time
Row B: Knit all stitches in pattern as established

You may not be able to perform all of the cable crosses in certain rows due to your decreases. Do not panic, work your decreases and knit or purl your stitches near the decreases. No one will ever know that you could not cross your cables.

Repeat rows A & B until 18 stitches remain. Cut yarn and kitchener the stitches together. Weave in ends and block.

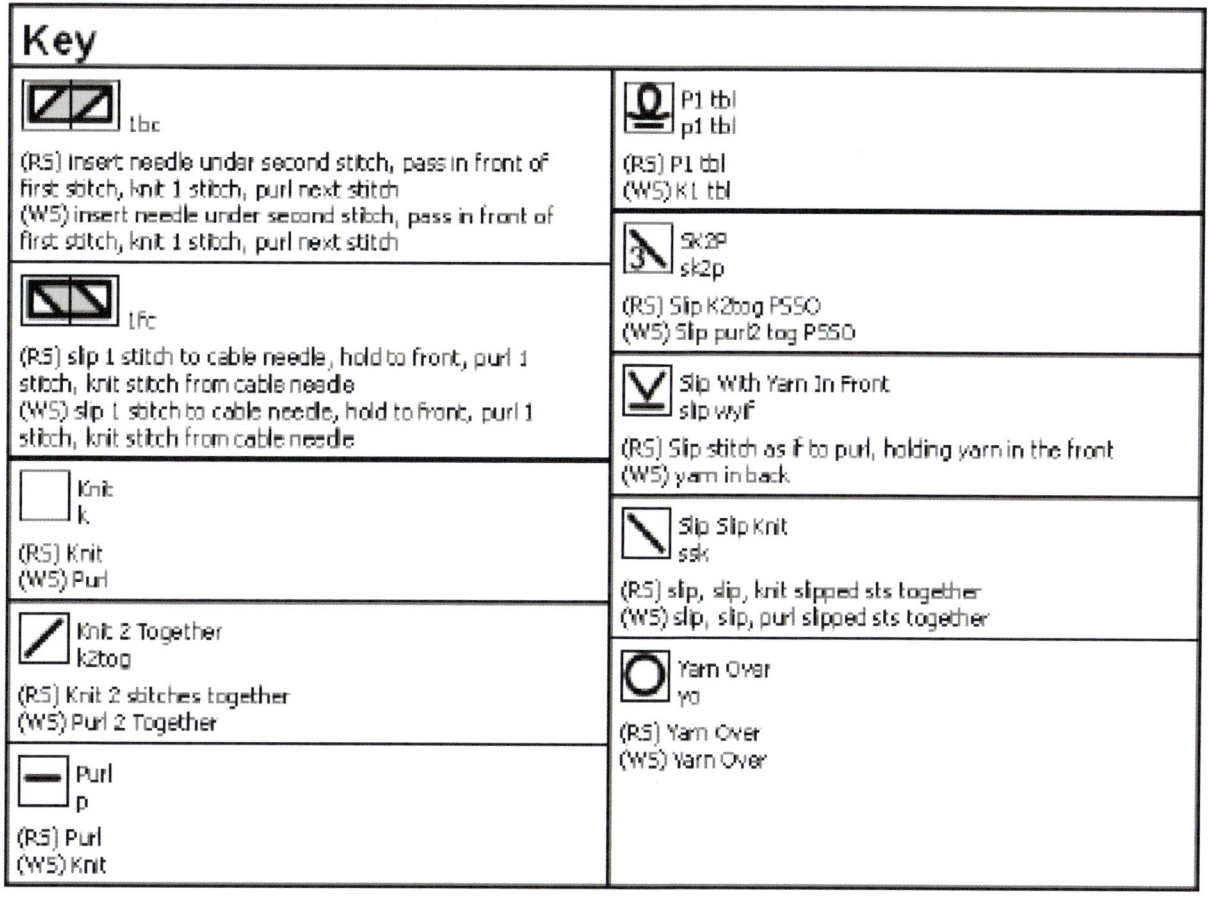

Honeybee Sock

Foot Chart

29	28	27	26	25	24	23	22	21	20	19	18	17	16	15	14	13	12	11	10	9	8	7	6	5	4	3	2	1	
				−	−		−	−		−	−		−	−		−	−		−	−		−	−						8
				−	−		−	−		−	−		−	−		−	−		−	−		−	−						7
				−	−	▨	▨	▨	▨	▨	▨	▨	▨	▨	▨	▨	▨	▨	▨	▨	▨	−	−						6
				−	−		−	−		−	−		−	−		−	−		−	−		−	−						5
				−	−		−	−		−	−		−	−		−	−		−	−		−	−						4
				−	−		−	−		−	−		−	−		−	−		−	−		−	−						3
				−	−	▨	▨	▨	▨	▨	▨	▨	▨	▨	▨	▨	▨	▨	▨	▨	▨	−	−						2
																													1

Hoppy Feet ~ A Year of Socks

June's Pattern: Honeycomb Tea Cozy

Honey and tea go so well together. When I had a bit of yarn leftover from my Honeybee socks, I decided that I needed to make a little something else to go with them. What better pairing than a tea cozy in the honeycomb pattern to match your socks? Put on a cuppa and enjoy your cozy socks with a nice warm pot of tea.

Skill level: This pattern is meant for a novice to advanced knitter. Please read the entire pattern before beginning.

Yarn: 1 skein Broken Pattern Bamboo Sock, 430 yards, 60% Merino, 30% Bamboo, 10% Nylon (~90 yards needed for the pattern/ 24 grams)

Needle: US 1 (2.25 mm) Hiya Hiya Circular needle or needles to obtain gauge

Gauge: 7.25 stitches per inch (spi) and 9 rows per inch (rpi) OR 29 stitches & 36 rows to 4 inches/10 cm in stockinette

Size: 6.5 inches tall, 11 inches around in a relaxed state. Approximately 15 inches around when stretched onto the teapot.

To alter the size: Adjust your gauge to increase or decrease the tea cozy as needed or add repeats of the honeycomb pattern.

To Begin:

Cast-on 54 stitches.

Row 1: s1, *p1, k2, p1, repeat from * to end of row, end k1
Row 2: s1, *k1, p2, k1, repeat from * to end of row, end p1

Repeat rows 1 and 2 for one inch.

Honeycomb Pattern:

Row 1: s1, *knit row 1 of honeycomb chart, repeat from * to end of row, end k1
Row 2: s1, *knit row 2 of honeycomb chart, repeat from * to end of row, end p1

Repeat rows 1 and 2 for three inches

Honeycomb Chart:
Row 1 (rs): 1bc, 1fc
Row 2 (ws): p1, k2, p1
Row 3 (rs): k1, p2, k1
Row 4 (ws): p1, k2, p1
Row 5 (rs): 1fc, 1bc
Row 6 (ws): k1, p2, k1
Row 7 (rs): p1, k2, p1
Row 8 (ws): k1, p2, k1

Shaping:

Row 1: s1, ssk, *knit in pattern as established, repeat from * to end of row, k2tog, end k1
Row 2: s1, p2tog, *knit in pattern as established, repeat from * to end of row, p2togtbl, end p1

Repeat rows 1 and 2 for 2.5 inches. Your tea cozy half should be 6.5 inches tall. Bind off. (I had 10 stitches left when I bound off)

Make 2 pieces alike. Sew side seams of the 2 pieces together, leaving space for the handle and spout.

Note: If your teapot is larger than mine, you may add stitches in 4 repeat increments and knit the honeycomb pattern for longer to extend the size.

Honeycomb Chart

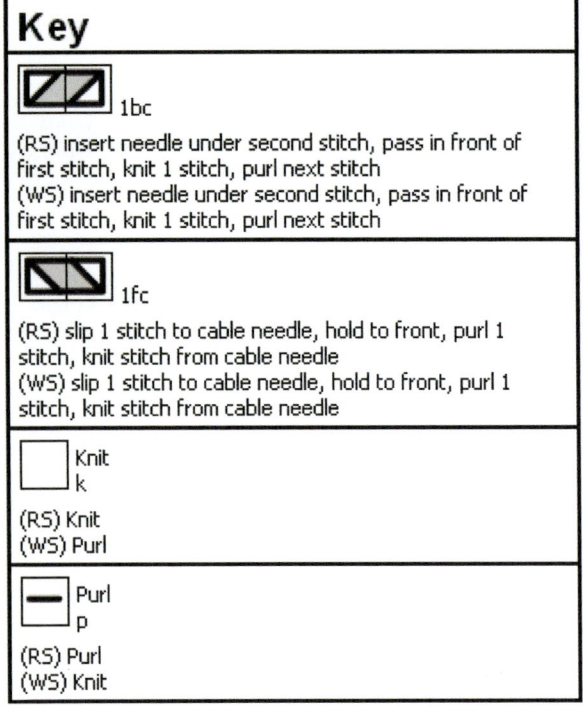

Fireworks Socks

July's Pattern: Fireworks Socks

This month's Hoppy Feet Sock focuses on the little details, starting with the Knitted On Cast-On. This Cast-On allows the knitter more control over use of the yarn as it is started with a short tail instead of a long tail. The 2 by 2 ribbed cuff is simple, but a classic ribbing and lends beautiful lines to the cuff.

Stockinette was my choice of fabric for the leg as it made a lovely canvas for the embroidered fireworks. The plain stockinette leg fabric leads into a stockinette heel as well before we work the band heel. I rather like the band heel in this sock. It is not a heel that I work very often, but it lends sophistication to an otherwise simple sock.

The stockinette fabric continues down the foot of the sock, but without the embroidered fireworks that are seen on the leg. You could always add a few stitches if you wanted though!

The toe is a spiral toe, but I like to think of it as a swirling nebula. Nebulas are made of stars and this toe is what I think of when I hear the phrase "star toe." So, I've referred to it as both in my pattern. It lends yet another small detail to the sock to make it special.

When deciding on the embroidery for the sock, I chose traditional fireworks. My favorite fireworks are the ones that shoot straight into the night sky, burst into a fountain of lights, and then sparkle with small stars. I chose to represent these fireworks on my socks. You may use the diagrams I have provided to stitch my favorite fireworks or make your own.

Techniques

Knitted-On Cast-On
Band Heel
Star Toe
Embroidery

Skill level: This pattern is meant for an adventurous novice to intermediate knitter. Please read the entire pattern before beginning.

Yarn: 1 skein Lilliput Yarns Simple Sock, 400 yards, 100% Superwash Merino, Fire Hydrant

Needle: US 1 (2.25 mm) Signature Steel Double Pointed Needles (DPNs) or needles to obtain

Gauge: 7.5 stitches per inch (spi) and 10 rows per inch (rpi) OR 30 stitches & 40 rows to 4 inches/10 cm in stockinette

Size: To fit a US women's 8.5-9 shoe, approx. 8.5" circumference and 9" foot

Notions: Tapestry needle and 3 yards of yarn in blue and white

To alter the size: Adjust your gauge to increase or decrease the circumference of the foot as needed.

Abbreviations: See the back of the book.

To Begin Socks:
Using the Knitted Cast-on, cast-on 56 stitches. You may want to mark the beginning of your round with a stitch marker, bit of floss, or waste yarn.

Sock Cuff:
Establish the sock cuff ribbing: *P1, K2, P1,* repeat from * to * around the sock. Continue in established pattern for 1 inch.

Leg:
Continue by knitting every stitch until the leg measures 7 inches from cast-on edge or to desired length.

Band Heel:
The heel is worked over the first 28 stitches of the row. Hold the remaining 28 stitches for the top of the foot. Remember to slip the first stitch of each row.

Row 1: S1, K27
Row 2: S1, P27

Repeat rows 1 and 2 until heel flap measures 2 inches long. Then start heel turn.

Heel Turn Part 1:
Row 1: S1, K8, K2tog, K6, SSK, K9 (26 stitches)
Row 2, 4, 6, 8: S1, purl to end
Row 3: S1, K7, K2tog, K6, SSK, K8 (24 stitches)
Row 5: S1, K6, K2tog, K6, SSK, K7 (22 stitches)

Heel Turn Part 2:
Row 1: K13, SSK, turn work (21 stitches)
Row 2: S1, P6, P2tog, turn work (20 stitches)
Row 3: S1, K6, SSK, turn work (19 stitches)
Row 4: S1, P6, P2tpg, turn work (18 stitches)

Repeat rows 3 & 4 five more times. There will be 8 stitches left.

Gusset:
Knit the 8 stitches of the heel turn. Pick-up and knit 12 stitches along band heel flap, pm, knit across 28 stitches for top of foot, pm, then pick-up and knit 12 stitches along the other side of the heel flap. Knit 4 stitches of band heel turn, PM. This is now the beginning of the row.

Gusset decreases:
Row A: Knit to 3 stitches before marker, K2tog, K1, SM, knit to next marker, SM, K1, SSK, knit to beginning of round marker.
Row B: Knit all stitches.

Repeat rows A & B one more time. There are 56 stitches again.

Foot:
Continue working foot by knitting every row until foot measures 7.5 inches from heel or to desired length. Stop your foot 1.5 inches from your total desired length. Remove all stitchmarkers except for the beginning of round marker.

Spiral Toe:
Row A: *K6, k2tog, pm, repeat from * 6 more times
Row B: Knit all stitches
Row C: *Knit until 2 stitches before marker, k2tog, repeat from * 6 more times
Row D: Knit all stitches

Repeat rows C & D until 7 stitches remain. Cut yarn, run through all stitches, and pull tight. Weave in ends and block.

Using a tapestry needle and contrasting blue and white yarns, embroider the fireworks on the socks. I have included some diagrams for your use or just free-hand the design. Remember to weave in your ends on the back side and avoid knots as they will rub when the sock is worn.

Fireworks Sock

Fireworks Diagram

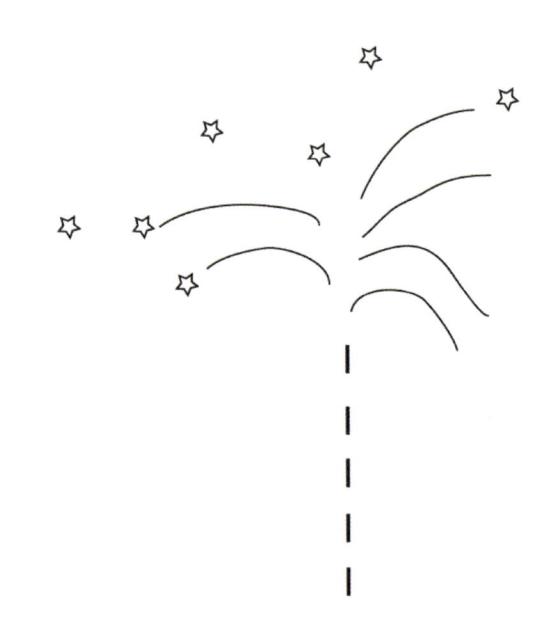

The socks depicted have a slightly different pattern on each leg. One sock has four stars, the other has seven. This is to show you that you may put as many or few stars on the sock as you like. Have fun with your design. Match them or mis-match them!

It Never Stays In Vegas Socks

August's Pattern: It Never Stays In Vegas Socks

It's time to have some fun with your socks! This pattern is meant to be completely at the mercy of the die. You roll your die to determine which of six lace patterns to include on the next color stripe of your sock. Each pattern is a die face. So as you roll you add the die face to your socks. It is a bit silly, but oh, so much fun. You can match your socks or leave them crazy. Just remember, it never stays in Vegas!

The Twisted German Cast-On is one of my favorite ways to start a sock. We have used this Cast-On twice before, but it gives such a nice edge that I had to use it again. The sock cuff is a comfortable 2 x 2 ribbing, the same ribbing I used in the July sock.

From the cuff, we transition into a random lace pattern. With the included die you roll the die to determine the pips. The number of pips translates into the lace pattern you use. There are 6 faces to a die and 6 patterns to use. So, if I rolled a 3 for the first pattern, I would use Die Chart 3. You continue to roll the die and knit the faces as presented. It's your own little Vegas game.

I chose a French Heel for this sock which uses a plain stockinette heel flap. The plain heel flap is a nice contrast to the striped and patterned leg. I then chose to knit the foot plain so that the stripes were highlighted down the foot. The colors that we chose for the socks should remind you of poker chips. Dice on the leg and poker chips on the foot. It's a real Vegas experience.

To finish the socks, I chose a pointed toe. This is a toe we have not tried before and is an interesting toe with delayed decreases. It fits very differently than the other toes we have worked. Work your toe and try it on. Do you like how it fits?

Techniques

Twisted German Cast-On
French Heel
Pointed Toe
Randomized Pattern
Lace

Skill level: This pattern is meant for an adventurous novice to intermediate knitter. Please read the entire pattern before beginning.

Yarn: 1 skein Lilliput Yarns Simple Sock, 400 yards, 100% Superwash Merino

Needle: US 1 (2.25 mm) Signature Steel Double Pointed Needles (DPNs) or needles to obtain gauge

Gauge: 7.5 stitches per inch (spi) and 10 rows per inch (rpi) OR 30 stitches & 40 rows to 4 inches/10 cm in stockinette

Size: To fit a US women's 8.5-9 shoe, approx. 8.5" circumference and 9" foot

To alter the size: Adjust your gauge to increase or decrease the circumference of the foot as needed.

Abbreviations: See the back of the book.

To Begin Socks:
Using the Twisted German Cast-on, cast-on 56 stitches. You may want to mark the beginning of your round with a stitch marker, bit of floss, or waste yarn.

Sock Cuff:
Establish the sock cuff ribbing: *P1, K2, P1,* repeat from * to * around the sock. Continue in established pattern for 1 inch.

Leg:
If you are using long stripe sock yarn follow this section, if not, skip to the next paragraph. Knit every stitch until your yarn transitions to the next color. Stop at the "start of round" stitchmarker. Don't worry if your color does not start exactly at the stitchmarker.

It's time to have some fun with this sock. Grab your die and roll. Which number do you have? Write it down here _____. You will use this number to determine which lace chart to follow in the leg pattern.

Establish the leg pattern:

##
Row 1: *Follow row 1 of Die Lace Chart _____, k 7, pm (or sm).* Repeat from * to * 3 more times.
Row 2: *Follow next row of Die Lace Chart _____, k7, sm.* Repeat from * to * 3 more times.

Repeat row 2 of the leg pattern until all rows of the Die Lace Chart have been worked.

If you are using long stripe sock yarn, knit every stitch until your yarn transitions to the next color. Stop at the "start of round" stitchmarker. Don't worry if your color does not start exactly at the stitchmarker. Roll your die to determine which lace chart to follow. Write it down here _____.

Row 1: *K7, follow row 1 of Die Lace Chart _____, sm.* Repeat from * to * 3 more times.
Row 2: *K7, follow next row of Die Lace Chart _____, sm.* Repeat from * to * 3 more times.

Repeat row 2 of the new leg pattern until all rows of the Die Lace Chart have been worked.

If you are using long stripe sock yarn, knit every stitch until your yarn transitions to the next color. Stop at the "start of round" stitchmarker. Don't worry if your color does not start exactly at the stitchmarker. Roll your die to determine which lace chart to follow.

Write it down here _____.##

Continue to follow the pattern as established from ## to ## until the leg measures 7.5 inches from cast-on edge or to desired length.

Heel:
The heel is worked over the first 28 stitches of the row. Hold the remaining 28 stitches for the top of the foot. Remember to slip the first stitch of each row.

Row 1: S1, K27
Row 2: S1, P27

Repeat rows 1 and 2 until heel flap measures 2 inches long. Then start heel turn.

Heel Turn:
Row 1: S1, K15, SSK, K1, turn work.
Row 2: S1, P5, P2tog, P1, turn work
Row 3: S1, Knit to one stitch before gap, SSK, K1, turn work.
Row 4: S1, Purl to one stitch before gap, P2tog, P1, turn work.

Repeat rows 3 & 4 until all of the stitches have been worked. On the final repeat of rows 3 & 4, skip the K1 and P1 at the ends of the rows. Knit across row. There will be 16 stitches left.

Gusset:
Pick-up and knit 11 stitches along heel flap, pm, knit across 28 stitches for top of foot, pm, then pick-up and knit 11 stitches along the other side of the heel flap. Knit 8 stitches of heel turn, PM. This is now the beginning of the row.

Gusset decreases:
Row A: Knit to 3 stitches before marker, K2tog, K1, SM, knit to next marker, SM, K1, SSK, knit to beginning of round marker.
Row B: Knit all stitches.

Repeat rows A & B until there are 56 stitches left.

Foot:
Continue working foot by knitting every row until foot measures 7 inches from heel or to desired length. Stop your foot 2 inches from your total desired length.

Star Toe:
Divide the stitches into four equal sections, and place new stitchmarkers. Remove the old side stitchmarkers.

It Never Stays in Vegas Sock

Row A: *K7, SSK, knit to stitchmarker, repeat from * 3 more times
Row B-D: Knit all stitches
Row E: *Knit until 2 stitches before marker, SSK, repeat from * 3 more times

Repeat rows A through D twice. Then repeat row A 4 times. Then repeat row E until 4 stitches remain. Cut yarn, run through all stitches, and pull tight. Weave in ends and block.

Die Chart 1 (Written):
Round 1: p7
Round 2: p1, k5, p1
Round 3: p1, k5, p1
Round 4: p1, k5, p1
Round 5: p1, k2, yo, k2tog, k1, p1
Round 6: p1, k5, p1
Round 7: p1, k5, p1
Round 8: p1, k5, p1
Round 9: p7
Round 10: k7

Die Chart 2 (Written):
Round 1: p7
Round 2: p1, k5, p1
Round 3: p1, k5, p1
Round 4: p1, k3, yo, k2tog, p1
Round 5: p1, k5, p1
Round 6: p1, k5, p1
Round 7: p1, k1, yo, k2tog, k2, p1
Round 8: p1, k5, p1
Round 9: p7
Round 10: k7

Die Chart 3 (Written):
Round 1: p7
Round 2: p1, k5, p1
Round 3: p1, k3, yo, k2tog, p1
Round 4: p1, k5, p1
Round 5: p1, k2, yo, k2tog, k1, p1
Round 6: p1, k5, p1
Round 7: p1, k1, yo, k2tog, k2, p1
Round 8: p1, k5, p1
Round 9: p7
Round 10: k7

Die Chart 4 (Written):
Round 1: p7
Round 2: p1, k5, p1
Round 3: p1, k5, p1
Round 4: p1, k1, yo, k2tog, yo, k2tog, p1
Round 5: p1, k5, p1
Round 6: p1, k1, yo, k2tog, yo, k2tog, p1
Round 7: p1, k5, p1
Round 8: p1, k5, p1
Round 9: p7
Round 10: k7

Die Chart 5 (Written):
Round 1: p7
Round 2: p1, k5, p1
Round 3: p1, k1, yo, k2tog, yo, k2tog, p1
Round 4: p1, k5, p1
Round 5: p1, k2, yo, k2tog, k1, p1
Round 6: p1, k5, p1
Round 7: p1, k1, yo, k2tog, yo, k2tog, p1
Round 8: p1, k5, p1
Round 9: p7
Round 10: k7

Die Chart 6 (Written):
Round 1: p7
Round 2: p1, k5, p1
Round 3: p1, k1, yo, k2tog, yo, k2tog, p1
Round 4: p1, k5, p1
Round 5: p1, k1, yo, k2tog, yo, k2tog, p1
Round 6: p1, k5, p1
Round 7: p1, k1, yo, k2tog, yo, k2tog, p1
Round 8: p1, k5, p1
Round 9: p7
Round 10: k7

Die Chart 1

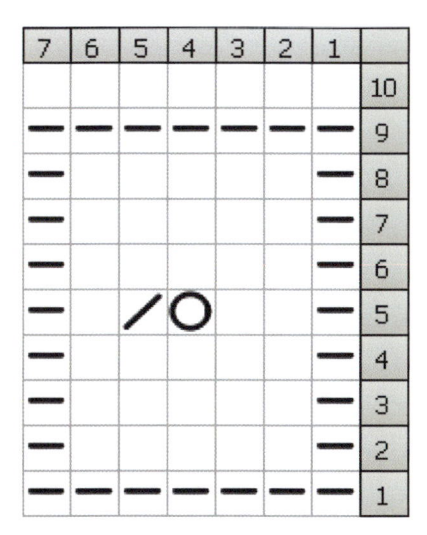

7	6	5	4	3	2	1	
							10
—	—	—	—	—	—	—	9
—						—	8
—						—	7
—						—	6
—			/	O		—	5
—						—	4
—						—	3
—						—	2
—	—	—	—	—	—	—	1

Die Chart 2

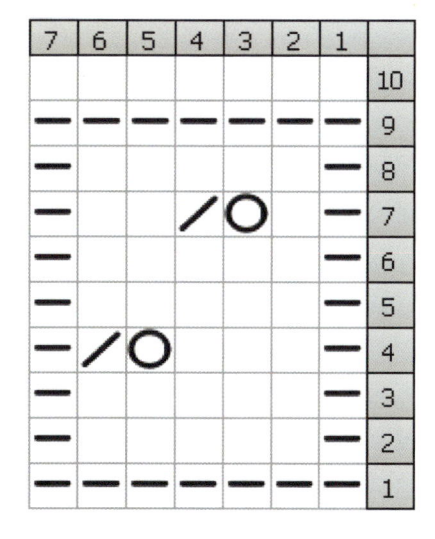

7	6	5	4	3	2	1	
							10
—	—	—	—	—	—	—	9
—						—	8
—		/	O			—	7
—						—	6
—						—	5
—			/	O		—	4
—						—	3
—						—	2
—	—	—	—	—	—	—	1

Die Chart 3

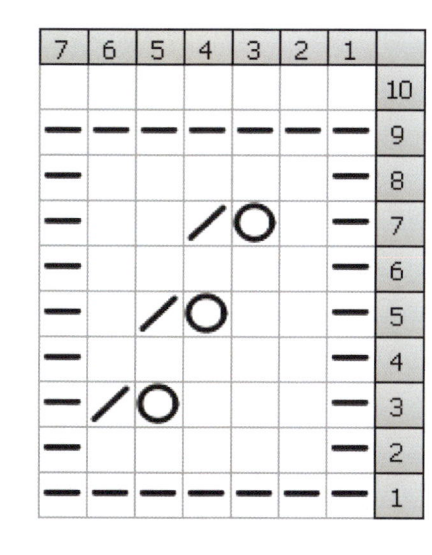

7	6	5	4	3	2	1	
							10
—	—	—	—	—	—	—	9
—						—	8
—		/	O			—	7
—						—	6
—		/	O			—	5
—						—	4
—			/	O		—	3
—						—	2
—	—	—	—	—	—	—	1

Die Chart 4

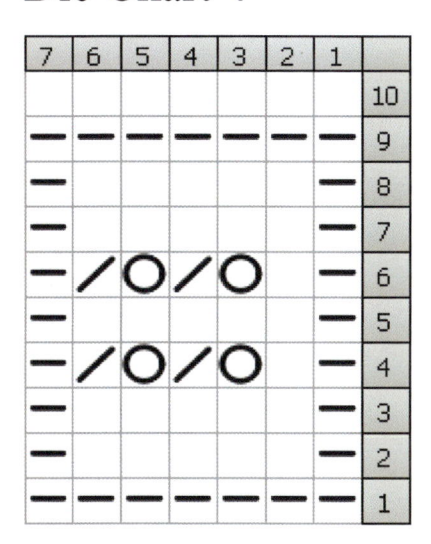

7	6	5	4	3	2	1	
							10
—	—	—	—	—	—	—	9
—						—	8
—						—	7
—	/	O	/	O		—	6
—						—	5
—	/	O	/	O		—	4
—						—	3
—						—	2
—	—	—	—	—	—	—	1

Die Chart 5

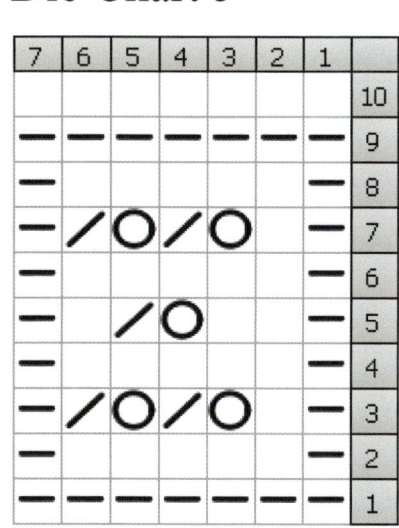

7	6	5	4	3	2	1	
							10
—	—	—	—	—	—	—	9
—						—	8
—	/	O	/	O		—	7
—						—	6
—			/	O		—	5
—						—	4
—	/	O	/	O		—	3
—						—	2
—	—	—	—	—	—	—	1

Die Chart 6

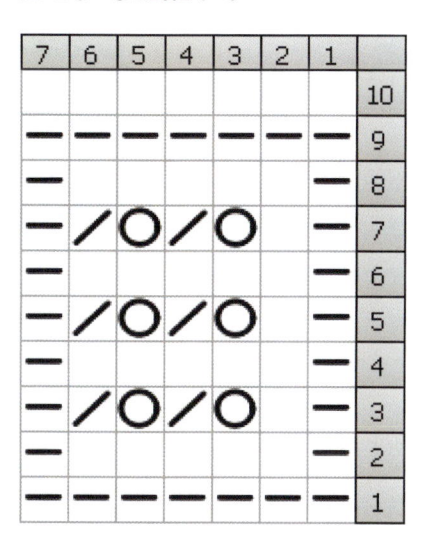

7	6	5	4	3	2	1	
							10
—	—	—	—	—	—	—	9
—						—	8
—	/	O	/	O		—	7
—						—	6
—	/	O	/	O		—	5
—						—	4
—	/	O	/	O		—	3
—						—	2
—	—	—	—	—	—	—	1

Key

☐	Knit / k / (RS) Knit (WS) Purl
/	Knit 2 Together / k2tog / (RS) Knit 2 stitches together (WS) Purl 2 Together
—	Purl / p / (RS) Purl (WS) Knit
O	Yarn Over / yo / (RS) Yarn Over (WS) Yarn Over

It Never Stays in Vegas Sock

Chicken Little Socks

September's Pattern: Chicken Little Socks

Our travels through sock techniques take us to the Long Tail Cast-On in September. This is a standard cast-on taught to many knitters as their first or second cast-on. It provides a solid edge from which to work your project without too much difficulty.

Once again, I have chosen K1, P1 ribbing for the cuff. K1P1 ribbing hugs very well and gives a clean line to the top of the sock. Our pattern is worked off-center to allow it to flow along the outside edge of the leg and onto the top of the foot.

Be careful as you are working the puff stitch pattern to ensure that you are dropping your YO's on the following row. This allows the knit stitches to elongate and "puff" out which creates our eggs in our Chicken Little pattern. I hope that the lace ribbing reminds you of chicken tracks, as it does for me.

Our heel is worked over half of the available stitches and is an Eye-of-Patridge patterned slip stitch heel. This heel is both squishy and reinforced thanks to the yarn that floats behind the fabric.

We continue the egg and chicken tracks pattern down the foot until we come to the toe. This toe is similar to a round toe, but uses delayed decreases to change the shape into a wider toe. This type of toe is particularly nice for those people with shorter toes and wider feet.

Pay careful attention to the sequence of the rows in the wide toe and the number of stitches between decreases.

Techniques

Long-Tail Cast-On
Patterned Heel Flap
Wide Toe
Puff Stitch
Lace

Skill level: This pattern is meant for an adventurous novice to intermediate knitter. Please read the entire pattern before beginning.

Yarn: 2 skeins Think Bamboo Superwash Sock Yarn, 224 yards, 40% Wool, 45% Rayon from Bamboo, 15% Nylon, color 9910

Needle: US 1 (2.25 mm) Signature Steel Double Pointed Needles (DPNs) or needles to obtain gauge

Gauge: 8.5 stitches per inch (spi) and 12 rows per inch (rpi) OR 34 stitches & 48 rows to 4 inches/10 cm in stockinette

Size: To fit a US women's 8.5-9 shoe, approx. 8.5" circumference and 9" foot

To alter the size: Adjust your gauge to increase or decrease the circumference of the foot as needed.

Abbreviations: See the back of the book.

Chicken Little Sock

To Begin Socks:
Using the Longtail Cast-On, cast-on 62 stitches. You may want to mark the beginning of your round with a stitch marker, bit of floss, or waste yarn.

Sock Cuff:
Row 1: *K1, P1, repeat from * until end of round.

Repeat row 1 until the cuff measures 1 inch in length. You will now make the determination to knit either the right sock or the left sock. One is a mirror image of the other.

Right Charted Leg:
The leg is now divided into 2 sections. The first 31 stitches are the back of the leg and the last 31 stitches are the front of the leg. Starting with set-up row you will follow the chart row, k 12 stitches, repeat the same chart row, k12. You will knit each repeat twice (once for the front and once for the back), but you will only knit the set-up rows one time.

Row 1: *Knit row 1 of chart, k12, repeat from * once.
Row 2: *Knit row 2 of chart, k12, repeat from * once.

Establish the sock leg pattern as follows:

Row 3: *Knit row 3 of chart, k12, repeat from * once.
Rows 4-10: *Knit next row of chart, k12, repeat from * once.

You will repeat rows 3-10 of the chart for your pattern repeat. Continue knitting the leg in pattern until the leg measures 7 inches from cast-on edge or to desired length. Slip all markers as you come to them, if used.

Right Written Leg:
The leg is now divided into 2 sections. The first 31 stitches are the back of the leg and the last 31 stitches are the front of the leg. Starting with set-up row you will follow the Chicken Little Pattern row, k 12 stitches, repeat the same Chicken Little Pattern row, k12. You will knit each repeat twice (once for the front and once for the back), but you will only knit the set-up rows one time.

Row 1: *Knit row 1 of Chicken Little Pattern, k12, repeat from * once.
Row 2: *Knit row 2 of Chicken Little Pattern, k12, repeat from * once.

Establish the sock leg pattern as follows:

Row 3: *Knit row 3 of Chicken Little Pattern, k12, repeat from * once.
Rows 4-10: *Knit next row of Chicken Little Pattern, k12, repeat from * once.

You will repeat rows 3-10 of the chart for your pattern repeat. Continue knitting the leg in pattern until the leg measures 7 inches from cast-on edge or to desired length. Slip all markers as you come to them, if used.

Chicken Little Pattern:
Round 1: p2, k5, p2, k1, p2, k5, p2
Round 2: p2, k5, p2, k1, p2, k5, p2
Round 3: p2, k2tog, yo, k1, yo, ssk, p2, inc4, p2, k2tog, yo, k1, yo, ssk, p2
Round 4: p2, k5, p2, k1 elongated3, k1, p2, k5, p2
Round 5: p2, k5, p8, k5, p2
Round 6: p2, k5, p2, k1 elongated3, k1, p2, k5, p2
Round 7: p2, k2tog, yo, k1, yo, ssk, p8, k2tog, yo, k1, yo, ssk, p2
Round 8: p2, k5, p2, p4tog, p2, k5, p2
Round 9: p2, k5, p2, k1, p2, k5, p2
Round 10: p2, k5, p2, k1, p2, k5, p2

Left Charted Leg:
The leg is now divided into 2 sections. The first 31 stitches are the back of the leg and the last 31 stitches are the front of the leg. Starting with the set-up row you will follow the chart row, k 12 stitches, repeat the same chart row, k12. You will knit each repeat twice (once for the front and once for the back), but you will only knit the set-up rows one time.

Row 1: *K12, knit row 1 of chart, repeat from * once.
Row 2: *K12, knit row 2 of chart, repeat from * once.

Establish the sock leg pattern as follows:

Row 3: *K12, knit row 3 of chart, repeat from * once.
Rows 4-10: *K12, knit next row of chart, repeat from * once.

You will repeat rows 3-10 of the chart for your pattern repeat. Continue knitting the leg in pattern until the leg measures 7 inches from cast-on edge or to desired length. Slip all markers as you come to them, if used.

Right Written Leg:
The leg is now divided into 2 sections. The first 31 stitches are the back of the leg and the last 31 stitches are the front of the leg. Starting with set-up row you will follow the Chicken Little Pattern row, k 12 stitches,

repeat the same Chicken Little Pattern row, k12. You will knit each repeat twice (once for the front and once for the back), but you will only knit the set-up rows one time.

Row 1: *K12, knit row 1 of Chicken Little Pattern, repeat from * once.
Row 2: *K12, knit row 2 of Chicken Little Pattern, repeat from * once.

Establish the sock leg pattern as follows:

Row 3: *K12, knit row 3 of Chicken Little Pattern, repeat from * once.
Rows 4-10: *K12, knit next row of Chicken Little Pattern, repeat from * once.

You will repeat rows 3-10 of the chart for your pattern repeat. Continue knitting the leg in pattern until the leg measures 7 inches from cast-on edge or to desired length. Slip all markers as you come to them, if used.

Heel:
The heel is worked over the first 31 stitches of the row. Hold the remaining 31 stitches for the top of the foot.

Eye of Patridge Heel Pattern:
Row 1: *S1, K1,* repeat from * to * across row, end K1
Row 2: S1, purl across row
Row 3: S1, K1, *K1, S1, * repeat from * to * across row, end K1
Row 4: S1, purl across row

Repeat rows 1 through 4 eight times or until heel flap measures two inches long.

Heel Turn:
Row 1: S1, K16, SSK, K1, turn work.
Row 2: S1, P4, P2tog, P1, turn work
Row 3: S1, Knit to one stitch before gap, SSK, K1, turn work.
Row 4: S1, Purl to one stitch before gap, P2tog, P1, turn work.

Repeat rows 3 & 4 until all of the stitches have been worked. **Note that you will not have enough stitches for the final k1 on the last right side decrease row or P1 on the last wrong side decrease row.** Knit across row. There will be 17 stitches left.

Gusset:
Pick-up and knit 17 stitches along heel flap, pm, knit in established pattern across 31 stitches for top of foot, pm, then pick-up and knit 17 stitches along the other side of the heel flap. Knit 9 stitches of heel turn, PM. This is now the beginning of the row.

Gusset decreases:
Row A: Knit to 3 stitches before marker, K2tog, K1, SM, continue in leg pattern as established, SM, K1, SSK, knit to beginning of round marker.
Row B: Knit in pattern as established.

Repeat rows A & B until there are 62 stitches left.

Foot:
Continue working the foot by knitting in the pattern as established (patterned top of foot with stockinette sole) until foot measures 7 inches from heel or to desired length. Stop your foot 2 inches from your total desired length.

Toe:
Remove beginning of round marker. Knit 15 stitches. Place beginning of round marker. This is now the beginning of your toe.

Row A: K3, SSK, knit until 5 stitches before marker, K2tog, K3, SM, K3, SSK, knit until 5 stitches before beginning of round marker, K2tog, K3.
Row B, C, D: Knit one round plain.

Repeat rows A-D 2 total times, then rows A-C 3 times, then rows A & B until toe measures approximately two inches, or to desired length, ending with row B.

Kitchener stitch the last 18 stitches together. Weave in ends and block.

Chicken Little Sock

Leg Chart

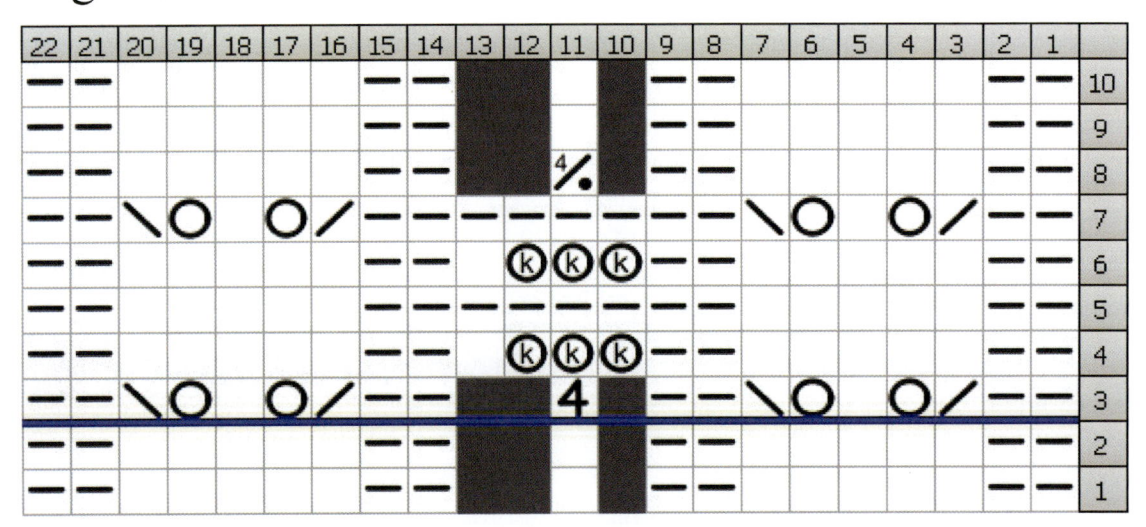

22	21	20	19	18	17	16	15	14	13	12	11	10	9	8	7	6	5	4	3	2	1	
—	—					—	—	■	■		■	■	—	—					—	—		10
—	—					—	—	■	■		■	■	—	—					—	—		9
—	—					—	—	■	■	⁴⁄.	■	■	—	—					—	—		8
—	—	\	O		O	/	—	—	—	—	—	—	—	—	\	O		O	/	—	—	7
—	—					—	—		ⓚ	ⓚ	ⓚ		—	—					—	—		6
—	—					—	—						—	—					—	—		5
—	—					—	—		ⓚ	ⓚ	ⓚ		—	—					—	—		4
—	—	\	O		O	/	—	—	■	■	4	■	—	—	\	O		O	/	—	—	3
—	—					—	—	■	■		■	■	—	—					—	—		2
—	—					—	—	■	■		■	■	—	—					—	—		1

Rows 3-10 are repeat rows

Rows 1 and 2 are Set-up Rows

Key

4 inc4
(RS) Increase 4 stitches in 1 stitch. K1, P1, K1, P1

Knit
k
(RS) Knit

ⓚ K1 Elongated
k1 elongated
(RS) knit and yarn over. yarn over to be dropped on following row

/ Knit 2 Together
k2tog
(RS) Knit 2 stitches together

— Purl
p
(RS) Purl

⁴⁄. Purl 4 Together
p4tog
(RS) Purl 4 Together

**** Slip Slip Knit
ssk
(RS) slip, slip, knit slipped sts together

■ No Stitch
x
(RS) No Stitch

O Yarn Over
yo
(RS) Yarn Over

Drifting Leaves Socks

October's Pattern: Drifting Leaves Socks

In further exploration of ways to start and end a sock, the Drifting Leaves socks are begun with a Double-Start Cast-On. This Cast-On is more flexible than a Long-Tail Cast-On. It pairs nicely with the 2 x 2 ribbed cuff.

From the cuff, the sock transitions into the drifting leaves pattern. The drifting leaves are worked in a series of increases to the widest point of the leaf and then decreased. This causes the stitch count to vary greatly as the leaf is worked. I found it very important to mark my drifting leaf with stitchmarkers. The leaves drift around the leg with the use of paired increases and decreases that cause the pattern to swirl.

Due to the nature of the leaf pattern, these socks are somewhat stretchy and extra comfortable. The leaves also puff a bit with the extra stitches in the fabric. I chose to maintain the rest of the sock in stockinette so that the knitter may increase or decrease the circumference of the sock without altering the pattern significantly.

An afterthought heel allows the knitter to continue knitting the sock without breaking for the heel. A line of waste yarn is knit into the sock until the toe has been worked.

The leaves continue to drift around the foot until the sock is long enough. Then a wedge toe is worked. Once the toe is kitchenered, the waste yarn is picked out and the stitches are placed back on needles. A "second toe" is worked over the picked up stitches to form the heel.

As you knit, the leaves will slowly drift around your foot until they rest beneath your toe. For those who would like to mirror their socks, I have included a basic instruction on the last page.

Techniques

Double Start Cast-On
Afterthought Heel
Wedge Toe
Textured

Skill level: This pattern is meant for an adventurous novice to intermediate knitter. Please read the entire pattern before beginning.

Yarn: 2 skeins Blue Ridge Yarns, Tango, 100% Superwash Merino Wool, 400 yards, Apple Rose

Needle: US 2 (2.75 mm) Hiya Hiya Steel Double Pointed Needles (DPNs) or needles to obtain gauge

Gauge: 6 stitches per inch (spi) and 9 rows per inch (rpi) OR 24 stitches & 36 rows to 4 inches/10 cm in stockinette

Size: To fit a US women's 8.5-9 shoe, approx. 8.25" circumference and 9" foot

To alter the size: Adjust your gauge to increase or decrease the circumference of the foot as needed.

Abbreviations: See the back of the book.

To Begin Socks:
Using the Double Start Cast-On, cast-on 48 stitches, join in the round, being careful not to twist. You may want to mark the beginning of your round with a stitch marker, bit of floss, or waste yarn.

Sock Cuff:
Row 1: *P1, K2, P1, repeat from * until end of round. Repeat row 1 until the cuff measures 1 inch in length.

Establish Leg Pattern:

If you have placed a stitch marker for the beginning of the round, place a second marker next to it. You will move this marker to indicate the pattern repeat. Our pattern repeat will shift around the leg as we knit.

To establish the leg: k1, knit row 1 of the Drifting Leaves Pattern (DLP) Chart, place end of pattern marker, knit to end of row.

Row A: Knit to 1 stitch prior to the DLP, K1, work RLI, work next row of DLP, SSK, knit to end of row.
Row B: Knit all stitches prior to DLP, work next row of DLP, knit to end of row.

Repeat Rows A & B until the leg measures 7 inches.

NOTE: The stitch count changes dramatically within each repeat of the DLP. There are 7 stitches in the first row of the DLP.

Drifting Leaves Pattern:
Round 1: p3, p1, p3
Round 2: p3, p1, p3
Round 3: p3, p1, p3
Round 4: p3, k1, p3
Round 5: p3, inc3, p3
Round 6: p3, k3, p3
Round 7: p3, pfb, k1, pfb, p3
Round 8: p3, k5, p3
Round 9: p3, pfb, k3, pfb, p3
Round 10: p3, k7, p3
Round 11: p3, pfb, k5, pfb, p3
Round 12: p3, k9, p3
Round 13: p3, ssk, k5, k2tog, p3
Round 14: p3, k7, p3
Round 15: p3, ssk, k3, k2tog, p3
Round 16: p3, k5, p3
Round 17: p3, ssk, k1, k2tog, p3
Round 18: p3, k3, p3
Round 19: p3, k3tog, p3
Round 20: p3, p1, p3

Afterthought Heel Set-up:
Now you will add in waste yarn to hold stitches for the Afterthought Heel. To do this, start at the beginning of the round and knit with the waste yarn for 24 stitches.

Foot:
Working over the waste yarn stitches, knit with your sock yarn again and continue in the pattern as established until the sock measures 12 inches from the cast-on edge or to desired length. Slip all markers (if used) as you come to them.

Toe:
The first 24 stitches will be the sole of your toe and the last 24 stitches will be the top of your toe. Place a stitchmarker after the first 24 stitches to mark the transition.

Row A: *K1, SSK, knit to 3 stitches before stitchmarker/end of needle K2tog, K1, repeat from * 1 more time
Row B: Knit all stitches

Repeat rows A & B until 16 stitches remain. Cut yarn and kitchener the stitches together.

Afterthought Heel:

Slide a needle through 1 loop of each stitch along the waste yarn on each side. Make sure to pick-up 24 stitches along each side of the waste yarn plus 2 additional stitches on each side at the gap.

Drifting Leaves Sock

Drifting Leaves Pattern Chart

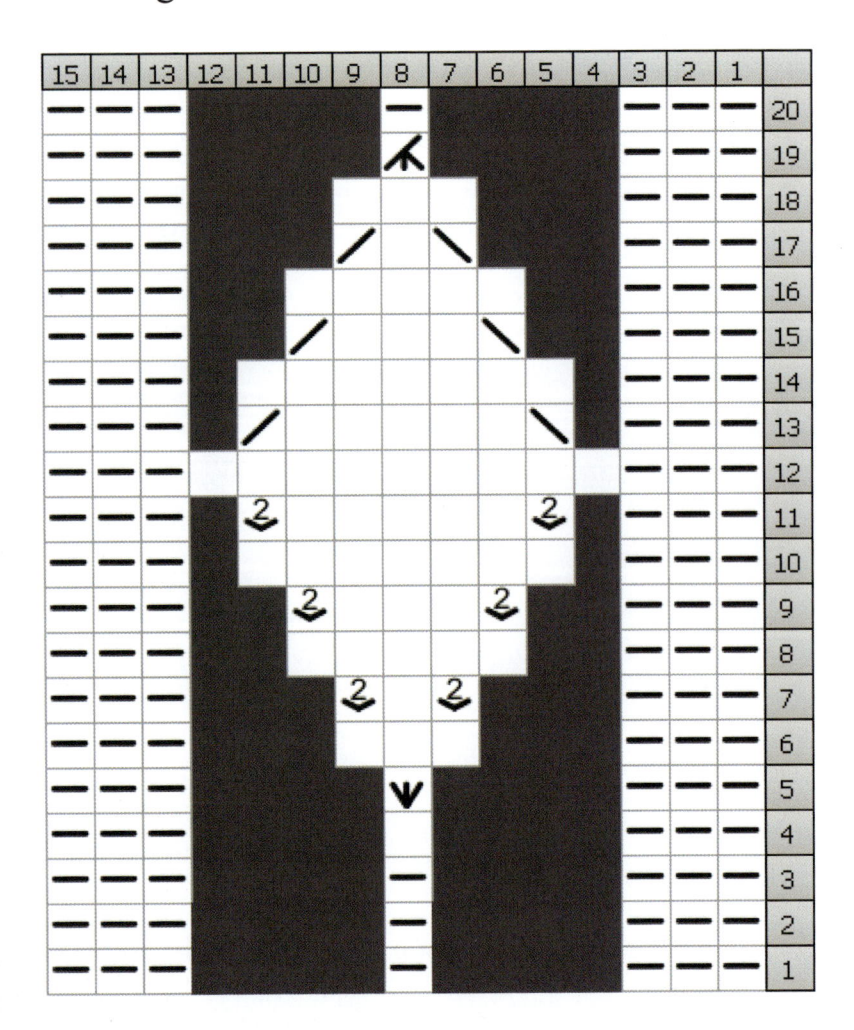

15	14	13	12	11	10	9	8	7	6	5	4	3	2	1	
–	–	–					–					–	–	–	20
–	–	–					⋏					–	–	–	19
–	–	–				/		\				–	–	–	18
–	–	–			/				\			–	–	–	17
–	–	–										–	–	–	16
–	–	–		/						\		–	–	–	15
–	–	–										–	–	–	14
–	–	–	/								\	–	–	–	13
–	–	–										–	–	–	12
–	–	–			2				2			–	–	–	11
–	–	–										–	–	–	10
–	–	–				2		2				–	–	–	9
–	–	–										–	–	–	8
–	–	–				2		2				–	–	–	7
–	–	–										–	–	–	6
–	–	–					ⱱ					–	–	–	5
–	–	–										–	–	–	4
–	–	–					–					–	–	–	3
–	–	–										–	–	–	2
–	–	–					–					–	–	–	1

Key

ⱱ	Increase 1-to-3 / inc3 — (RS) knit, purl, knit in 1 stitch / (WS) knit, purl, knit in 1 stitch
(blank)	Knit / k — (RS) Knit / (WS) Purl
/	Knit 2 Together / k2tog — (RS) Knit 2 stitches together / (WS) Purl 2 Together
⋏	Knit 3 Together / k3tog — (RS) Knit 3 stitches together / (WS) Purl 3 Together
2	Knit Front Back / kfb — (RS) Knit in Front and Back in same stitch / (WS) Purl in Front and Back in same stitch
–	Purl / p — (RS) Purl / (WS) Knit
\	Slip Slip Knit / ssk — (RS) slip, slip, knit slipped sts together / (WS) slip, slip, purl slipped sts together
■	No Stitch / x — (RS) No Stitch / (WS) No Stitch

On the first row, K2tog (1 gap stitch and 1 sole stitch), knit22, k2tog (1 gap stitch and 1 sole stitch), pm, k2tog (1 gap stitch and 1 top stitch) k22, k2tog (1 gap stitch and 1 top stitch). You should have 48 stitches remaining.

On next row follow Rows A & B below to decrease as you did for the toe. Essentially, you are creating two "toes" in your sock.

Heel Continued:

Row A: *K1, SSK, knit in pattern to 3 stitches before stitchmarker/end of needle K2tog, K1, repeat from * 1 more time
Row B: Knit all stitches in pattern

Repeat rows A & B until 16 stitches remain. Cut yarn and kitchener the stitches together. Weave in ends and block.

Note: To have mirrored socks, on the second sock: k2tog, work the DLP, then work a left lifted increase.

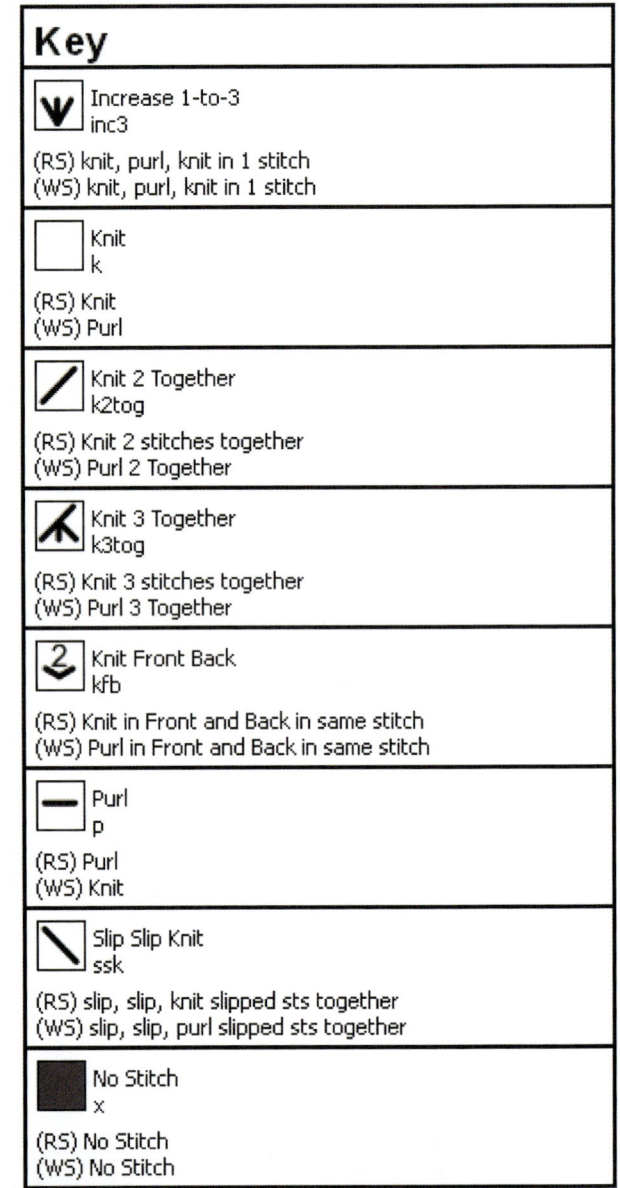

Armistice Socks

November's Pattern: Armistice Socks

When I considered our second to last sock for the BlackSheep Hoppy Feet Club, I knew that it needed to be meaningful. I chose to combine a German heel with a French toe and knit the sock in the color of the poppies that wave across the fields of Europe. Those same poppies which inspired the poem "In Flanders Field" during World War I. Combine all of these things with our November club offering and it results in the Armistice Socks.

Armistice Day is celebrated on November 11th and marks the day when the Allies and Germany signed a cessation of hostilities during World War I. When thinking about which sock to make in November, I decided to embrace this day of remembrance. I chose a German heel and a French toe as both countries participated in this coming together to end the war.

The Picot Cast-On that begins the Armistice Socks reminded me of poppy petals falling from the flowers. Once the poppy petals grace the top edge of your sock, it is a breeze to knit the knit one, purl one ribbing before transitioning into lovely smooth stockinette down the leg.

To continue the theme of Armistice Day, I chose a German heel for these socks. The German heel has a construction similar to a slip-stitch heel flap, but with purl bands instead of slipped stitches. The heel flows back into more stockinette before ending in a French Toe.

The French toe is similar in construction to a Spiral Toe; however, it uses paired decreases instead of a single decrease.

Techniques

Picot Cast-On
German Heel
French Toe

Skill level: This pattern is meant for an adventurous novice to intermediate knitter. Please read the entire pattern before beginning.

Yarn: 1 skein Colinette Jitterbug, 400 yards, 100% Superwash Merino Wool, color Fire

Needle: US 2 (2.75 mm) Signature Steel Double Pointed Needles (DPNs) or needles to obtain gauge

Gauge: 6.25 stitches per inch (spi) and 8 rows per inch (rpi) OR 25 stitches & 32 rows to 4 inches/10 cm in stockinette

Size: To fit a US women's 8.5-9 shoe, approx. 8.5" circumference and 9" foot

To alter the size: Adjust your gauge to increase or decrease the circumference of the foot as needed.

Abbreviations: See the back of the book.

To Begin Socks:
Using the Picot Cast-On, cast on 48 stitches.

Picot Cast-On:
1) Place a slip knot with a short tail on your left-hand needle.
2) Use the Knitted-On Cast-On to cast-on 4 more stitches (5 total)
3) Knit the first 2 stitches. Bind off 1 stitch. Knit 1 stitch. Bind off 1 stitch. Move the worked stitch back to the left-hand needle(2 stitches bound off and 3 left)
4) Cast on 4 stitches using the Knitted-On Cast-On.
5) Knit 2 stitches. Bind off 2 stitches. Pass the last worked stitch back to the left-hand needle.

Repeat steps 4 & 5 until you have 48 stitches on your needles. Join in the round being careful not to twist. You may want to mark the beginning of your round with a stitch marker, bit of floss, or waste yarn.

Sock Cuff:
Row 1: *K1, P1, repeat from * until end of round.

Repeat row 1 until the cuff measures 1 inch in length.

Right Charted Leg:
Then knit every stitch and every row until the leg measures 7 inches from the top of the cuff or to desired length.

Heel:
The heel is worked over the first 24 stitches of the row, plus 6 more (30 total). Hold the remaining 18 stitches for the top of the foot.

Heel Pattern:
Row 1: S1, K24, P2, K2
Row 2: S1, P24, K2, P2

Repeat rows 1 and 2 eleven times, or until heel measures 2 inches long.

Heel Turn:
Row 1: S1, K1, P2, K12, SSK, turn work.
Row 2: S1, P2, P2tog, turn work
Row 3: S1, Knit to gap, SSK, turn work.
Row 4: S1, Purl to gap, P2tog, P1, turn work.

Repeat rows 3 & 4 until all of the stitches have been worked. Knit across row. There will be 16 stitches left.

Gusset:
Pick-up and knit 11 stitches along heel flap, pm, knit 18 stitches for top of foot, pm, then pick-up and knit 11 stitches along the other side of the heel flap. Knit 8 stitches of heel turn, PM. This is now the beginning of the row.

Gusset decreases:
Row A: Knit to 3 stitches before marker, K2tog, K1, SM, continue in leg pattern as established, SM, K1, SSK, knit to beginning of round marker.
Row B: Knit in pattern as established.

Repeat rows A & B until there are 48 stitches left.

Foot:
Continue working the foot by knitting until the foot measures 7.5 inches from heel or to desired length. Stop your foot 1.5 inches from your total desired length.

Toe:
Remove beginning of round marker. Knit 15 stitches. Place beginning of round marker. This is now the beginning of your toe.

Row A: *K1, SSK, k10, K2tog, K1, SM,* repeat from * to * two more times (3 times total).
Row B: Knit all stitches

Repeat rows A & B until 12 stitches remain. Run your yarn through all of the stitches and pull titghtly. Weave in ends and block.

Armistice Sock

Snowflake Christmas Stocking

December's Pattern: Snowflake Christmas Stocking

With the Christmas Stocking, I chose a Chained-On Cast-On. This type of Cast-On allows for a sturdy edge for the rolled edge from the purl rows. The rolled edge gives the stocking a more substantial appearance and allows us to easily know where to attach the I-cord loop later.

From our rolled edge we then work a few rows plain before beginning the colorwork section of the stocking. I chose a very traditional Swedish motif for this stocking and high contrast colors of red and white that remind me of Christmas and snow.

After completing the colorwork portion of the stocking, it is easy stockinette that takes us to the heel where we change colors. The white heel gives visual interest to the sock without being difficult to work. Adding in the red color once more when starting the gussets gives continuity to the sock.

The sock continues in stockinette until just before the toe where a simple colorwork checked stripe is added. The red yarn is then cut and the sock toe is knit in white yarn with a simple spiral toe to finish.

The I-cord loop is started by picking up stitches just beneath the edge of the purled cuff and knitting until it is long enough to loop comfortably. Using the tail, the loop is sewn down to the inside of the stocking just beneath the rolled brim, eliminating extra tails and bits to sew in.

Techniques

Chained-On Cast-On
Colorwork
Wedge Toe
Contrast Heel and Toe

When I thought about the last sock for this sock club, I knew that I wanted it to be a Christmas Stocking. I love Christmas and the memories of hot cocoa and frozen cookies dipped in the warm liquid. Christmas to me is best displayed in cheerful knitted stockings and the littlest gifts that were always hidden inside. I hope you will find this Christmas Stocking wrapped into your warmest memories of Christmases to come.

Skill level: This pattern is meant for an adventurous novice to intermediate knitter. Please read the entire pattern before beginning.

Yarn: 1 skein Lettlopi, 100% Icelandic Wool, 109 yards, color 9434 and 1 skein color 0051

Needle: US 6 (4 mm) Hiya Hiya Steel Double Pointed Needles (DPNs) or needles to obtain gauge

Gauge: 4.3 stitches per inch (spi) and 5 rows per inch (rpi) OR 17 stitches & 20 rows to 4 inches/10 cm in stockinette

Size: 10 inch circumference

To alter the size: Adjust your gauge to increase or decrease the circumference of the foot as needed.

Abbreviations: See the back of the book.

To Begin Socks:
Using the Chained Cast-on and red yarn, cast on 44 stitches. You may want to mark the beginning of your round with a stitch marker, bit of floss, or waste yarn.

Sock Cuff:
Purl 5 rows.

Leg:
Knit 8 rows. Then begin the Leg Chart.

Continue by knitting every stitch in red until the leg measures 10 inches from cast-on edge or to desired length.

Heel:
Change colors from red to white. The heel is worked over the first 22 stitches of the row. Hold the remaining 22 stitches for the top of the foot. Remember to slip the first stitch of each row.

Row 1: S1, K21
Row 2: S1, P21

Repeat rows 1 and 2 until heel flap measures 2.5 inches long. Then start heel turn.

Heel Turn:
Row 1: K12, SSK, K1, turn work.
Row 2: S1, P5, P2tog, P1, turn work
Row 3: S1, Knit to one stitch before gap, SSK, K1, turn work.
Row 4: S1, Purl to one stitch before gap, P2tog, P1, turn work.

Repeat rows 3 & 4 until all of the stitches have been worked. Knit across row. There will be 14 stitches left.

Gusset:
Knit the 14 stitches of the heel turn. Change yarn from white to red. Pick-up and knit 9 stitches along band heel flap, pm, knit across 22 stitches for top of foot, pm, then pick-up and knit 9 stitches along the other side of the heel flap. Knit 7 stitches of the heel turn, PM. This is now the beginning of the row.

Gusset decreases:
Row A: Knit to 3 stitches before marker, K2tog, K1, SM, knit to next marker, SM, K1, SSK, knit to beginning of round marker.
Row B: Knit all stitches.

Repeat rows A & B until there are 44 stitches remaining.

Foot:
Continue working foot by knitting every row until foot measures 7 inches from heel or to desired length.

Join in the white and work rows 1-5 of the Leg Chart. Cut the red, leaving a 4-5 inch tail.

Remove all stitchmarkers except for the beginning of round marker.

Continuing in white, work the toe as noted below.

Spiral Toe:
Row A: *K9, k2tog, pm, repeat from * 3 more times
Row B: Knit all stitches
Row C: *Knit until 2 stitches before marker, k2tog, repeat from * 3 more times
Row D: Knit all stitches

Repeat rows C & D until 8 stitches remain. Cut yarn, run through all stitches, and pull tight.

Using the white yarn, pick up and knit 4 stitches under the purl rim of the stocking on the heel side. Work I-cord for 6 inches (see note below). Then k2tog twice. Cut yarn, run through both stitches, and pull tight. Using the tail yarn, sew the i-cord down to the inside of the stocking.

Weave in ends and block.

Note: To work I-cord, use double pointed needles. Knit every stitch of the first row. Slide the stitches to the right end of the needle. Knit every stitch. Then repeat sliding and knitting until the cord is the desired length.

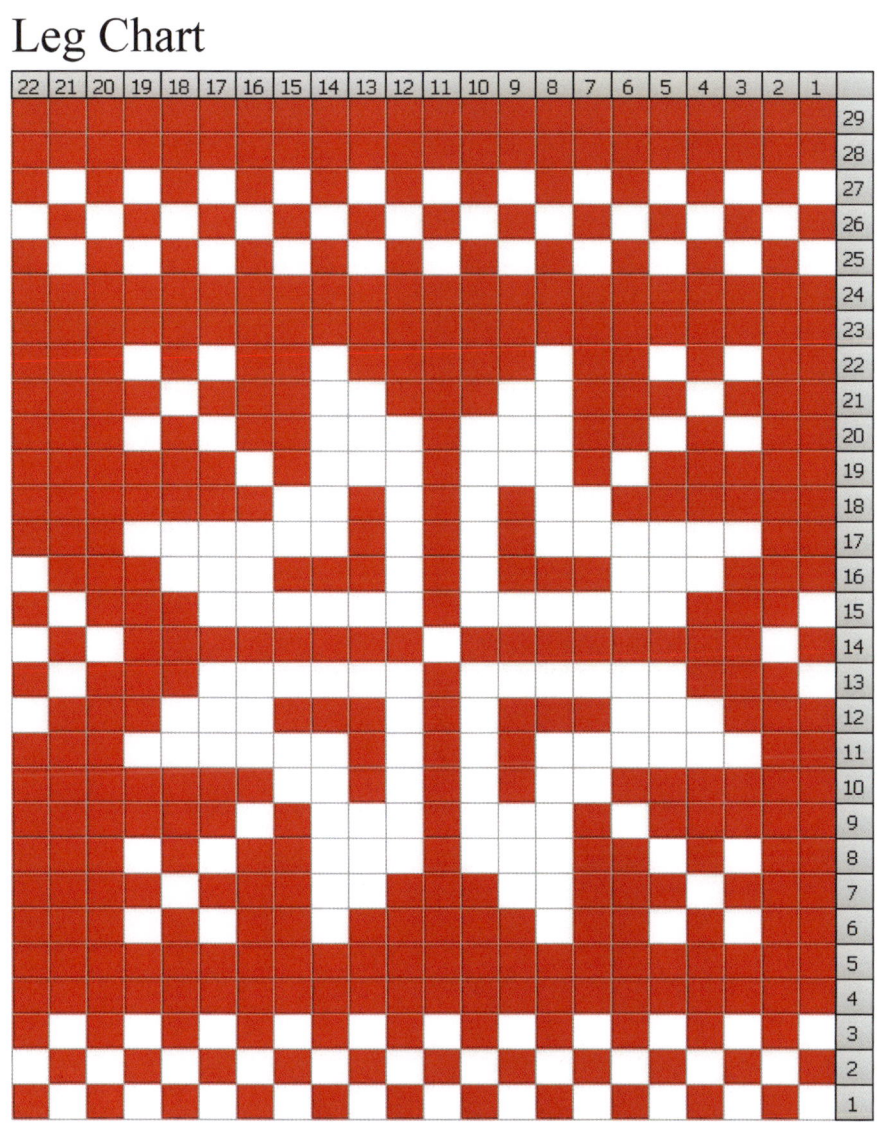

Leg Chart

Snowflake Christmas Stocking

About the Author

My designs are influenced by my family and friends in Indiana, as well as my time in the pacific northwest. I'm a triple graduate of Purdue University, though I don't hold a Doctorate. An avid reader, I am also a collector of needlework technique books, handkerchiefs, and tea. I learned to knit in the fall of 2002 and turned my thoughts to designing patterns in 2009. There are always ideas floating around my head, but only a few of them make it to the computer (aka my drawing board) and then on to a full pattern. It is my pleasure to present the first of what I hope will be many knitting pattern books for you to enjoy.

Are you looking for more of my patterns?
www.kellislackdesigns.com

Contact me at
kellislack@gmail.com

Abbreviations:

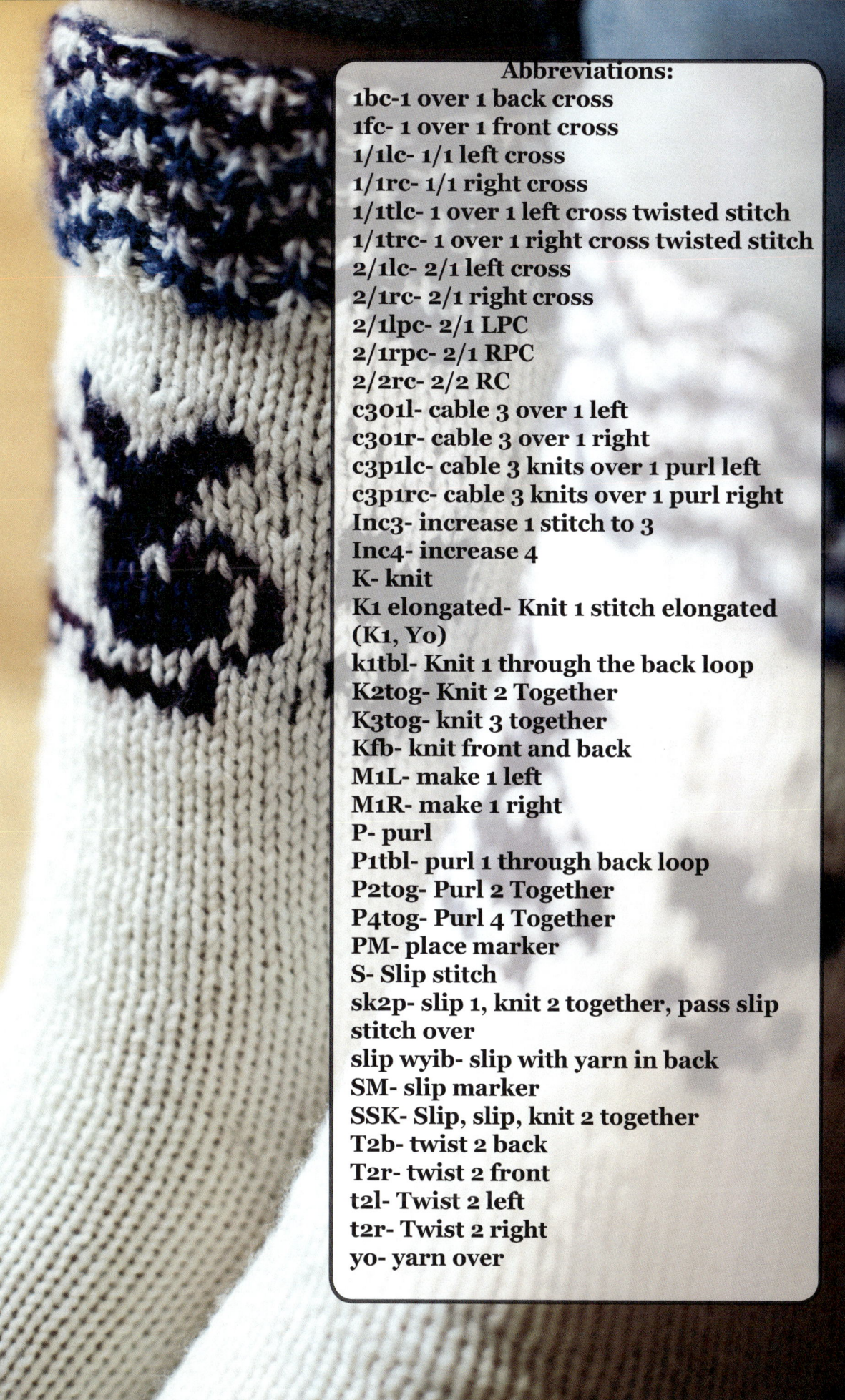

1bc- 1 over 1 back cross
1fc- 1 over 1 front cross
1/1lc- 1/1 left cross
1/1rc- 1/1 right cross
1/1tlc- 1 over 1 left cross twisted stitch
1/1trc- 1 over 1 right cross twisted stitch
2/1lc- 2/1 left cross
2/1rc- 2/1 right cross
2/1lpc- 2/1 LPC
2/1rpc- 2/1 RPC
2/2rc- 2/2 RC
c3o1l- cable 3 over 1 left
c3o1r- cable 3 over 1 right
c3p1lc- cable 3 knits over 1 purl left
c3p1rc- cable 3 knits over 1 purl right
Inc3- increase 1 stitch to 3
Inc4- increase 4
K- knit
K1 elongated- Knit 1 stitch elongated (K1, Yo)
k1tbl- Knit 1 through the back loop
K2tog- Knit 2 Together
K3tog- knit 3 together
Kfb- knit front and back
M1L- make 1 left
M1R- make 1 right
P- purl
P1tbl- purl 1 through back loop
P2tog- Purl 2 Together
P4tog- Purl 4 Together
PM- place marker
S- Slip stitch
sk2p- slip 1, knit 2 together, pass slip stitch over
slip wyib- slip with yarn in back
SM- slip marker
SSK- Slip, slip, knit 2 together
T2b- twist 2 back
T2r- twist 2 front
t2l- Twist 2 left
t2r- Twist 2 right
yo- yarn over

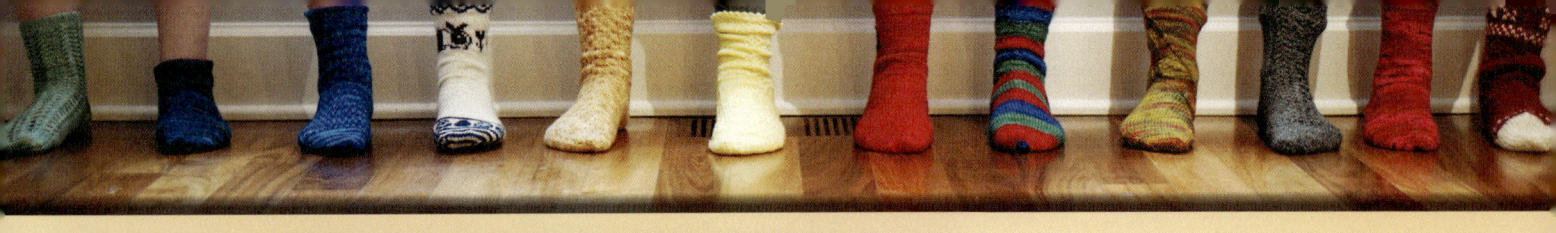

The Hoppy Feet Book is an exploration of all things sock. Whether you are new to socks or an old hand at turning heels, there is sure to be a delightful pattern in here for you. Throughout the book different cast-ons, bind-offs, heels, toes, textures, and techniques are used to highlight the delight that is a handknit sock. There is even a difficulty ranking to help you start your sock knitting journey. Whether your preference is toe-up or top-down, I hope you will join in the *Hoppy Feet* adventure and choose your sock!

Printed in Poland
by Amazon Fulfillment
Poland Sp. z o.o., Wrocław